THE MARRIAGE BOND

The
Marriage Bond

Helen Oppenheimer

THE FAITH PRESS
Leighton Buzzard, Beds, LU7 7NQ

PRINTED IN GREAT BRITAIN

in 10 point Times type

BY THE FAITH PRESS LTD.

LEIGHTON BUZZARD LU7 7NQ

SBN 7164 0455 9

TO
L.M.L-T AND H.M.L-T

PREFACE

THIS book came from an attempt to put into a coherent whole several articles which I had written on marriage and divorce for various periodicals over the last seven years. The earlier chapters have mostly been published before (with slight alterations); the later ones are mostly new.

I am grateful to the editors of the publications in which the articles appeared for permission to use the material again, as follows:

The account I wrote of *Marriage, Divorce and the Church* for 'See Round', the St. Albans Diocesan Leaflet, May, 1971, has become the Introduction.

'Marriage and Sex' from *The Franciscan* number on Morals in a Pluralist Society (June 1972) has become Chapter I and the end of Chapter IV.

'Marriage and Grace' from *Theology*, December 1969, considerably rewritten, has become Chapter III and the beginning of Chapter IV.

'Is the marriage bond an indissoluble *vinculum?*' part of a symposium with Mr. John Lucas and Professor Macquarrie, was originally written for the Anglican/Roman Catholic Commission on mixed marriages, and was printed in *Theology*, May 1975. It has become Chapter V.

'The Churches and Marriage' from *Concilium*, September 1973, has mostly been used in Chapter II and a little in Chapters VI, VII and VIII.

'Marriage, Divorce and the Church' from *Theology*, June 1971, was written as a reply to Mr. John Lucas's critique of the report. I have used it in Chapter VIII and the very end of Chapter V.

I owe many thanks, of which a few need special mention. Besides my husband, for help at all stages, I am particularly grateful to all the members of the 1969 marriage commission,

7

to whom the thought of this book is inextricably indebted; and to Mr. John Lucas, for friendly criticism. There is a wedding sermon by the late Austin Farrer, published in *A Celebration of Faith*, which says all that need really be said about marriage.

I am very happy to dedicate this book to my parents in the year of their golden wedding.

HELEN OPPENHEIMER

December 1975.

CONTENTS

INTRODUCTION

THIS book is not a treatise on marriage. It has a more limited aim, to discuss the theology of marriage in view of the difficulties created by the human fact of divorce. I have written as an Anglican and about conditions in England, because that is what I know at first hand, but if what I have tried to say is at all sound I hope it would be applicable more widely.

The Church of England has an honourable history of theological and humane thought on the understanding of marriage. It is fair to say that Anglicans have characteristically tried hard to obey Christ's teaching and to relate it to human life and fulfilment. They have not ignored his hard sayings nor been content to apply them in unimaginative rigorism. In relation to the State, the Church has not succumbed weakly to secular pressures nor drawn itself apart from the world, refusing responsibility to the nation at large.

Of course, neither its theological understanding nor its charity towards human beings has been perfect; nor indeed its public relations. Any institution which prides itself on moderation and comprehensiveness is particularly liable to misunderstanding from outside and muddled thinking within. It has all the more need for constant constructive scrutiny of its beliefs in the light both of tradition and of current conditions.

This scrutiny has lately been going on more strenuously than ever. Since the passing of the Matrimonial Causes Act of 1857 the Church has become increasingly aware of the dilemma with which it is faced. On the one hand the most obvious interpretation of the reported teaching of Christ would be that there simply is no such thing as divorce: those who attempt re-marriage are doing no more and no less than 'living in sin'. How then can the Church celebrate these empty ceremonies for them, or even allow them to come to

11

Communion unless they repent and separate? On this view it is irrelevant whether a person was 'innocent' or 'guilty' in the first marriage: he or she is still married and cannot be married again.

On the other hand it is plain to anyone with a spark of human feeling, let alone Christian charity, that such treatment of divorced people quickly becomes Pharisaical in just the sense which the main emphasis of Christ's teaching condemns. It is judging other people's spiritual state, not getting oneself into miserable moral muddles, that disqualifies one for the kingdom of Heaven. Of course sinners have to repent, but repentance cannot always include undoing the past, for often it cannot be undone.

Over the years the Church of England has arrived at a kind of working compromise in this difficulty. It has not settled down in the permissiveness which shuts its eyes to Christ's 'hard sayings', nor in the severity which follows out its own logic without checking it by seeing where it leads in human terms. The attempt has been made to witness to the urgency of Christ's teaching by refusing to celebrate the second marriages of divorced people in church; but at the same time those who embark upon second marriages have not after all been excommunicated. Some Anglicans have shamefacedly looked on this policy as an illogical but practically needful compromise; others have sought to justify it by recognizing that a second marriage is not precisely the same as living in sin but has a kind of legal validity. Moses allowed the safety-valve of divorce for human hardness of heart, and Christ did not repudiate Moses but pointed beyond him. So one comes to see divorced remarried people not exactly as unrepentant sinners but as imperfect human beings who need not be denied the grace of God. To go as far as this does involve the recognition that a second marriage is *something*: that it is not just an empty form. But it has still seemed inescapable that for the Church to go so far as to bless such marriages would be to go against Christ's express wishes.

The temptation to rest at this point could be very great indeed; but the position has not proved stable. The continued pressure of the 'permissive society' proves nothing either way, for developing contemporary thought can be 'progress' or it can be 'of the Devil' and a Christian has to discriminate, not automatically go with the stream nor automatically dig in his toes. But what should make him go on thinking is the unresolved question of what the Church is really refusing when it refuses to bless a second marriage after divorce. If it is always refusing to bless a sin, so well and good. But what about the situations where, even as a Christian, one cannot help being humanly glad that a divorced person is to remarry? If a remarriage can ever seem to be the best of evils', one cannot for ever escape the question of whether, in the situation which really exists, it could even be God's will. Or at least one must ask oneself whether in God's mercy some good may come of it? And if the answer to either of these questions could be yes, it does not seem a promising way to help people to find God's will and go on doing it, to repudiate them when they come and ask for His blessing, even if the repudiation is supposed to be only temporary. It is easy enough today to be married in a register office, and it carries little or no social stigma. If people come and ask to be married in church there is a good chance that they want in all seriousness just what they claim to want, God's blessing itself, however vaguely they understand this and however unready or even unwilling they are to put it into words. It is a heavy responsibility to turn them away; and it inevitably seems to imply that for all our talk about forgiveness, it is sins and errors over sex and only those which really put people beyond the pale.

It cannot be claimed that the answer is obvious, but the Church has now begun to take the question very seriously. It is very much to be hoped that the outcome will not be, and will not be seen as, a simple victory either for rigorist or for liberal. Each has insights the other often lacks; the rigorist a deep loyalty to God's will, and a refusal to be defeatist about what marriage can be made into; the liberal a willingness to let his understanding be improved by real life, and a refusal to put logic before people. Each on his own is a cardboard man. What the Church needs is people who

13

will be obedient to God's will without being possessive about it, and who will act in charity towards human beings without being sentimental about them. Christians have a great deal to say about the possibilities of marriage and they are not by any means finding the world entirely deaf and unresponsive. The object of the present book is to show that there is still the opportunity to offer the world not a misty ideal but a reality so definite and so attractive that there is room for the generous acknowledgment of exceptions which are rightly given special treatment.

WHAT IS MARRIAGE?

I

TOTAL COMMITMENT

THERE is a caricature, not yet extinct, of the Christian doctrine of marriage which may be definite but which certainly cannot be called attractive: that the Almighty invented what are called 'the facts of life' solely as an expedient for populating the world; that the sinfulness of human beings has taken up sex as an end in itself not a merely necessary means to an end; but that once the number of the elect is accomplished, pure and virtuous souls can breathe a sigh of relief and live in contented celibacy.

The 1662 Prayer Book appears to support this view unreservedly in placing first among the causes for which Matrimony was ordained 'the procreation of children', and going on to back this up by putting next the idea that marriage is 'a remedy for sin'. Companionship comes only third and the physical relationship for its own sake nowhere. One does not need to be particularly suspicious of traditional authority to identify a logical error here. It is as if one were told that school was ordained for a remedy against truancy, or even that property was ordained for a remedy against theft. This acknowledged, however, it is worth pointing out after all that even the 1662 presentation of marriage is not so black as it is painted. It *is* fertility which characterizes (not defines) marriage among human relationships; anthropologically not just in the minds of theologians the institution of marriage arises as a way of safeguarding the upbringing of human young; so it is neither unrealistic nor obscurantist to call procreation, from one aspect, the primary purpose of marriage. Further, it ought to be noticed that before offspring are referred to at all the 1662 service has already given the relational side of marriage a more than honourable mention, for matrimony has been presented as 'signifying unto us the

17

mystical union that is betwixt Christ and his Church'.

These considerations of what the Anglican Church has taught are not entirely peripheral to those who as twentieth century Christians want to relate their understanding of human marriage to Christian teaching as it has come to them. If this traditional main line were noticeably false to human experience, more than just one expendable theory of marriage would be impugned for them. Though Christians in a plural society are certainly not committed to take the 1662 Prayer Book as final and definitive for their understanding, they are committed to continue to measure their conclusions against a Christian as well as a human yardstick.

An obvious next move is 'back to the Bible', not in any fundamentalist spirit but because if the Bible is not on the main line of Christian tradition then it is hard to see what is. And here, if preconceptions will allow, one can find solid basis for a doctrine completely different from the caricature with which I began.

The reported teaching of Christ about marriage is neither negative nor obscure. There is no need to be a particularly conservative critic to detect authenticity in the story that when Christ was questioned about divorce he took the whole question of marriage back behind the law of Moses to the Creation. 'From the beginning of creation', according to Genesis, Christ's Bible and ours, ' "God made them male and female". "For this reason a man shall leave his father and mother and be joined to his wife, and the two shall become one." So they are no longer two but one.' [1] The authoritativeness of this renews the authority of the ancient myth, and places the unity of husband and wife at the centre of the Christian doctrine of marriage. Sex, then, is not a disreputable activity apart from its usefulness in populating the world: it is a God-given way of making two people one.

In this sort of context the modern controversy about what moral need there is to legalize sex relationships at all resolves itself, not into questions about the efficiency of birth control, but into questions about how much commitment such relationship properly demands. The Christian may well want to continue to insist on 'total commitment', and if so arguments about the nature and timing of the marriage ceremony become strangely peripheral. If 'sex without marriage' means 'sex without commitment' he is not being legalistic in objecting; if it means as much commitment as in marriage, he will wonder what the fuss is about and why not call it marriage; if it means some commitment but less than in marriage, he will need to argue his case for more, but he will not be tempted to base his conviction on some magic respectability conferred by a particular ritual and lacking without it, but on the Christian concept of 'one flesh', however he can interpret it. What he will need to argue is that the union of two lives which is marriage is an attainable and worthy ideal, which requires for its realization the kind of trust which the exclusiveness of marriage builds up.[2]

By what right can such a substantial theory be built upon one biblical text? Is this not old-style 'proof-text' fundamentalism, and fundamentalism of a dangerous selective kind? A satisfying defence cannot be found simply in the bandying of further texts, nor even in an elaborate defence of the authenticity of this one, but in the exhibiting of this way of thinking about marriage as a suitable part of the Christian understanding of human nature, and of a piece with the whole Christian attitude to the physical and spiritual character of the world.

Tentatively it may be propounded that *sex is 'for' the building up of that unique relationship, marriage, which has as its biological function the continuance of the race (providing the context for the birth and nurture of children) but which comes to have as great a value in its own right.* As *felix culpa* has been said of man's sin which gave rise to the Atonement, so at this humbler level one might say 'happy need' of children which has given rise to the possibility of this relationship. In other words, the significance of certain states of affairs can sometimes (a Christian will say, in God's providence) far outstrip what could have been predicted from the way they came about: a seeming by-product can take on an overwhelming importance of its own.

19

This presentation of marriage has a naïve look in at least two ways. First, how dare one say that marriage is 'for' the building up of relationship? Humanists and Christians alike are apt cautiously to stop short of the teleological. Humanists may ask the question, What benefit can be extracted from such and such a situation? and may give constructive answers, but will sheer off any idea that the benefit could have been put there for people to find. Christians on the other hand are ready to enquire, What did God command? but are shy to suppose that it could have been for human happiness that He commanded it. Yet if it makes sense to say traditionally that the end of man is to glorify God and enjoy Him for ever, it does not seem foolish to suppose that when human relationships are lived with not against the grain, they are capable of development in ways which enhance rather than limit human capacity to enjoy and to glorify. To say this kind of thing has been characteristic of the Anglican tradition of moral theology, and can take as an example the authoritative good sense of Bishop Butler. It does require that the love of one another can be continuous with the love of God rather than in rivalry to it; but there is much in the New Testament, including the two great commandments, to encourage Christians to believe that this is so.

Secondly, how dare one say that the relationship of marriage is 'unique'? To affirm this has not been intended by Christians merely sociologically. They have meant to announce their belief that marriage is *intrinsically* unique, not just that it is a kind of relationship with a certain recognizable character, but that it lays a particular claim upon those who enter into it which they are not at liberty to set aside. Their commitment to each other is to be complete, not in the sense of preventing other kinds of commitment to other people, but in the sense that nothing is held back.

The physical union is one aspect of this: not the whole but symbolic of the whole and helping to create it. It could be an example of what O. C. Quick years ago called 'the principle of representative dedication'.[3] He applied the principle to a few of the problematic concepts of human religion:

20

to the primitive idea of sacrifice, to the relationship of the sacred and the secular, and to the question of primitive prayer. What he suggested was that in each of these cases the difficulties are less if the explicit offering of one aspect of life is understood as a valid token for a complete offering. For example, 'religious' persons are not holier than others: 'In them as a representative part the holiness permeating every part of the society is expressed and made as it were self-conscious'. If we can take his principle and apply it to marriage we can say that in the physical union as a representative part the commitment of the whole of two lives is expressed and brought to life.

Married people are to join their lives for as long as they both shall live in such a way as to have no remainder of the same sort for anyone else. Here alone among human relationships a certain possessiveness is in place, a consciousness of mutual belonging, in which honouring involves making claims not leaving free. Something of this awareness of being claimed as a person is experienced in parenthood, but asymmetrically and temporarily. Only in marriage is the claim reciprocal, exclusive and developing.

These are lofty affirmations. It is no wonder that to many it sounds only naïve or presumptuous to be willing to affirm them. The present argument does not aspire to prove that they are true but to set them out, to offer them for inspection to see whether they can, so to speak, 'prove themselves'. Anyone who wants to take them up, and in particular anyone who wants to apply them to human life at large, will have to take responsibility for seeing that two conditions are met: that the positive doctrine shall be realistic, and that something morally satisfactory can be said about the casualties. These conditions must be kept in mind and will eventually have to be faced.

II

HUMAN INSTITUTION

THE only way in which a Christian understanding of marriage can be fully justified is by being self-justifying: by having a sufficient intrinsic convincingness that those concerned tend to say 'Yes. That is what marriage is like: at its best maybe, but in approachable reality, not as an unattainable ideal'. When Christians have experienced marriage in this way, it is tempting for them to feel that now they really have identified 'Christian marriage'. They stand here by the grace of God, their marriage indeed is a means of grace, and the bonds which unite them are supernatural.

Without wanting to decry these insights, I believe that to gather them together in this particular way can be the beginning of a seriously false emphasis; and I want to take the argument in a somewhat different and more humanistic direction, in the belief that the longest way round may be a more reliable way home to a Christian understanding. The previous Church of England Commission on Marriage had as its terms of reference 'to prepare a statement on the Christian doctrine of marriage'. This seemingly neutral phrase, it is not too fanciful to suggest, already encapsulates a theory. I should like to argue that to develop this theory is to find the proper emphasis for Christian teaching about marriage.

The phrase indicates that there is a Christian doctrine of marriage, obscured and fragmented maybe, but not lost among Christian divisions. On the other hand, and no less significantly because negative, it seems to reject another concept, to suggest that one need not spend one's efforts looking for something called 'the doctrine of Christian marriage'. To seize on to this negative is to make a considerable claim. It is not to deny that the expression 'Christian marriage' makes any kind of sense, but to refuse to put a certain sort of emphasis upon it. There is indeed the marriage of Christians. There is, according to one great stream of traditional thought, marriage as a Christian sacrament. There are Christian insights into the meaning of marriage. There are transforming developments in the institution of marriage brought out by such insights. But there is *not* an essential something called 'Christian marriage' different in kind from the marriage of Philemon and Baucis, and even from the marriage at Cana of Galilee.

The basis of this seemingly negative but essentially positive claim, I have already tried to suggest, is not an argument from silence but is biblical. Out of what could have been merely an argument about divorce there stands up like a signpost the statement that the 'one-flesh' union of marriage goes back to 'the beginning of the creation'.[1] Christ's teaching on marriage then is not about a new institution founded by himself but about the human union of man and woman which goes back to pre-history. Part of what is meant by humanity is the capacity for fidelity including sexual fidelity. This is not a grandiose idealistic statement about human morality, but a precondition for the possibility of social existence as human beings have established it. People who could not trust each other at all would be precisely 'inhuman'. Plenty of men and women are unfaithful, some radically so, and only a few are heroically faithful, but the point is that human beings are creatures to whom the concept of faithfulness is applicable.[2] They can aspire to it and expect it of one another: it is not too much to call faithfulness, at least in its more workaday forms, *characteristic* of human nature. Something may be said to have gone wrong when it is lacking. This fact is what has made it possible for the institution of marriage in its diverse but recognizable forms to develop in human societies. This human phenomenon, not something belonging to the Church as such, is the raw material for a 'Christian doctrine of marriage'. Lifelong marriage is a *norm* in human life, which means two things, that it is normal and that it sets a standard.

23

Ecumenically such a starting-point is promising, because it goes back further than the points of difference to which the Christian churches seem committed. As long as they go on discussing derivative problems of divorce as these have taken shape, however benevolently they conduct the argument, they can hardly help consolidating their disagreements. Catholics have held a clear theory and are in trouble about how to be merciful in practice. Protestants have been merciful in practice and are in trouble about how to justify this in theory. The Orthodox have tried to please the State. The Anglicans have tried to please everybody. All these are unfair statements with enough truth in them to ruin understanding. To try to reconcile the developed points of view they caricature is like trying to force flowers back into their seeds.

To try instead to go back to the beginning carries the risk that in the end one will only re-elaborate one's existing presuppositions. The exercise will be too much for any one person: which is all the more reason for making a start upon it. Of course the specific problems cannot be shelved for long, but perhaps one can hope to steal up on them from a different angle, even if one has to take for one's motto the words of the Irishman, 'If I wanted to go to Dublin, I shouldn't be starting from here'. What is needed is more than a readiness to see other people's points of view. It is an even more difficult readiness to look through 'points of view' at the fundamentals they are trying to understand. It is more than ten years since Hans Küng wrote [3] about Christian reunion in general: 'If Catholics and Protestants both try, while bearing each other in mind, to get closer and closer to their own standards, then (*since the standard is the same for both*) they and their basic standards must begin more and more to coincide with one another'. This faith that 'the gospel of Christ is but one' [4] is not proving easy to establish or apply. Sometimes it seems that ecumenical advance is only a more sympathetic understanding of each other's difficulties; but here and there, notably in eucharistic theology, something definite is happening.[5] It is surely worth approaching the theology of marriage in this way.

The assumption to be explored is that Christ's teaching on marriage was not a replacement but a reminder and a refreshment for a human understanding of marriage which potentially existed already, which can be summed up in the words, 'The two shall become one flesh'. This gives honourable recognition and indeed emphasis to the physical union, but is not to be limited to that. It 'probably originally described the new social unity that marriage effected'.[6] The stress is laid on the idea of two separate beings becoming somehow one.

The whole point is that this concept is familiar. It can be the foundation of a doctrine of marriage because enough people have experienced marriage in this way to understand what the doctrine means. But once marriage is placed in this way in *human* life, it is fair to point out that unity-in-plurality is a concept familiar throughout Christian theology: [7] the concept of a union which is not a confusion nor a blending, which is more than harmony but more complex than mathematical oneness. The Christian faith is full of 'mysteries of coinherence',[8] in which separate beings are supposed to be united yet still distinct, joined together without being swamped or lost. From the Trinity to the grace of God in our own lives we have to learn to look for kinds of unity which in Teilhard de Chardin's phrase will 'differentiate' [9] not destroy. 'Three Persons in one God', 'Abide in me and I in you', 'I but not I': these are what Christianity is about, and seen in this light 'The two shall become one flesh' seems to be a kind of homely example illuminating the obscurity of these others and in turn capable of being illuminated by their profundity.

A Christian seems to catch a glimpse which is not just a will-o'-the-wisp of a homogeneous creation in which the same structures, so to speak, are rebuilt at many levels; and presently it will be useful to spell out in more detail what this can mean.[10] But first the point needs to be reiterated that the foundation of this whole line of thought is a human understanding of a human institution which existed and was valid before there was a Christian Gospel at all. Otherwise no analogy can get started. Christian theologians may rejoice that the human model is available to help elucidate divine mysteries; but if they move on to the divine too quickly without stopping to appreciate the human, they will only nip in the bud their comprehension of both marriage and theology.

If this emphasis is convincing, it follows that the proper attitude for the Churches to take up towards marriage is appreciative rather than defensive. Their role is not so much to witness as to welcome, to 'celebrate' in the fullest sense. In a different meaning of 'witness' though their role is precisely that; not to uphold marriage against possible attackers, but to be present in God's name when two people marry each other. This approach is consonant with the Catholic understanding of marriage as a sacrament. It has long been insisted that the ministers of the sacrament are the bride and bridegroom, that it is indeed as a witness that the priest is there.

Heart-searchings are going on at the moment in the Church of England about the fact that people have a legal right to be married in their parish church even when they never normally set foot there. On the present view it is neither weak nor hypocritical to set such anxieties aside and offer such people God's grace and blessing with whole-hearted rejoicing. There need be no element of pretence here, and it is not for us to try to judge the element of waste. If the cup into which one tries to pour something is too small, it will overflow: but all human vessels are too small. The Church is not 'going through the motions' of an unbelieved rite, making people mouth what they do not mean. It is doing for them what they have asked, allowing them to take each other as husband and wife 'in the presence of God and in the face of this congregation'. To take each other as husband and wife is a humanly, indeed a legally, valid act, not a hollow show. The law of England still means by it something very like what the Church means, the voluntary union for life of one man with one woman, not a contract dissoluble at the mere will of the parties.[11] If people still want to do this solemn act in church, however inarticulate they may be about what it means to them, it smacks of meanness and possessiveness for Christians to try to ration God's blessing. It must be faced that often people's

26

motivation will not only appear but will be decidedly inadequate. So maybe was the motivation of the prodigal son. He came home only when he wanted something he could not get elsewhere; yet his Father came to meet him.

Nor should churchmen belittle the extent to which people may be looking, even unawares, for something 'spiritual' although they are too shy to show it; and the most extrovert people are often the shyest about religion. If encouragement and enthusiasm are what they find when they approach the Church about their real human concerns, they are far more likely to be able to recognize the grace and blessing of God when it is offered to them.[12] It is not altogether easy for the clergy to comprehend how far in some quarters religion has become an unmentionable subject today, in the way in which sex is supposed to have been in the last century. Here is an occasion both natural and happy where this taboo on piety is apt to weaken. Should it not be seized upon, not for instant evangelism but for building up less timid attitudes?

Even where the happy couple's attitude is impenetrably social, it can still be worth showing that Christians are capable of rejoicing with those who rejoice, without nagging about divorce or even snatching greedily at 'pastoral opportunities'. Unless there is open scorn it is more appropriate to think of the rain falling alike upon the just and the unjust than of pearls being cast before swine. At least there is a chance for their families and friends to pray for people who are getting married, and for everyone present to see that something significant is happening. This joining of two lives is humanly important in the way that birth and death are important. The sacred and the secular meet here whether those concerned are pious or impious. This is what the Church is claiming when it is present in God's name at a wedding.

III

WORKING MODEL

IF marriage is a basic human institution not a Christian discovery, it does not follow that the Church has no business with it except to stand encouragingly by. The Church is concerned in God's name with the whole of human existence. Even if the task of regulating were entirely given up to the State, the task of interpreting would remain. I believe that this turns out to be a two-sided and analogical task, going to and fro between the divine and the human and tracing parallel problems in the way the world is and the things Christians say. The pursuit of analogies, of recurrent patterns in theology and nature, is a promising enterprise if the world is indeed, as I have tried to suggest,[1] a 'homogeneous creation'.

Why after all do people find the Christian understanding of marriage difficult? All the practical problems come sooner or later to one question: how can we believe that two can become one while still remaining two? But this question is not peculiar to marriage; the theme of unity-in-plurality haunts Christian theology. It sounds unconvincing that distinct persons could be united, really united not just harmoniously allied, without losing their separate identities, but much basic Christian doctrine requires that it should be so. Christianity has some strange things to say about God and His relationships with mankind. The doctrine of the Trinity sets forth three persons in one God; the 'immanence' of God means that He is in us and we in Him; the doctrine of Christ requires that Jesus should be one with God and yet a man, and that his death and resurrection somehow encompass us all; the doctrine of grace has encouraged us to believe that when God acts in us we are most truly ourselves. If 'unity in plurality' is incoherent, then Christianity itself is incoherent;

if it makes sense, it should illuminate large areas of human experience.

This possibility of illumination is what a Christian ought to expect. Christians affirm that the universe is the Creation and that theology is the truth about God's purposes for it. They should not be surprised to find that the sorts of things they believe about God find echoes in the experience they already have of human life, nor to find that these help to explain one another. This is in no way a new discovery. The most famous and characteristic of these recurrent patterns, the theme of death and rebirth, is authoritatively announced in the New Testament.[2] Another almost as fundamental and of special relevance to marriage is the sacramental theme, of which more must be said presently.[3]

The analogical approach welcomes these patterns and tries to trace them more clearly. It consists of starting with what we know, that is with what we find in human existence; applying it to what we have been told, that is the Christian doctrines about God and His dealings with mankind; and hoping eventually to look at human life again in the light of any insights we have gained, so that by moving cautiously and tentatively we begin to see a whole world view take shape, in which human and divine understanding will turn out to be of a piece with one another. To cherish this kind of hope is to refrain from cutting off the divine from the human, to refuse to insist prematurely upon the uniqueness of God when statements about Him seem contradictory. It is too easy to make a virtue of bafflement, to utter paradoxes glibly. Rather than asserting in cheerful defeatism that God is beyond our comprehension so nothing need be said about Him, it is more constructive to start instead with what is not beyond our comprehension and approach in cautious reverence as far as we can. So we need not postulate the uniqueness of God as a desperate expedient to save our doctrine, but can reach it at whatever stage in the argument it forces itself upon us as a

29

fact. Admittedly, such an approach is 'anthropomorphic'; but if man is made in God's image it seems wise to see how far this image will take us and only jettison it when it begins to crumble, not just for fear that it might.

The basis of this analogical approach is *personalism*. Persons are what matter and what matters about persons is their capacity for relationships with one another: this might be called a fundamental article of faith. So I should want to affirm that what matters about God, so to say, is that He is personal. This is the likeness we are asserting when we say that man is made in God's image. We know that human beings are personal beings, capable of relationships: we hope that in this they are small-scale working models of the infinite God, showing each other (though in a partial and distorted way) what He is like. So when the difficult and paradoxical statements of our faith are propounded to us, we can look first at human beings in relation to one another, to see if we can discern like paradoxes in familiar existence.

So, for example, if we are trying to understand grace, and asking how our wills can become one with God's without the loss of our identities, we may profitably enquire into known situations where some such unity appears to be a practical possibility, with the hope of understanding better both the human situation and the theology. Perhaps in human existence there is already to be found a greater complexity, indeed a greater mysteriousness, than is sometimes supposed, a sufficient complexity and mysteriousness to take us a stage further on the way towards understanding the reality of God without treating paradox as a refuge.

It may be said, Is this whole approach broken-backed? Is it just trying naïvely to meet the difficulties which arise out of God's *un*likeness to human beings and the *un*likeness of our relationships with Him to human relationships, by obstinately comparing God with human beings all over again? That is not quite what is being attempted. The suggestion is rather that the best way to begin to understand difficult statements about God and His dealings with us is by trying to enlarge our understanding of human beings and human relationships[4] and in particular by learning to realize that the simple picture of persons as separate distinct islands is not adequate even on a human level.

I have attempted this exercise more elaborately elsewhere.[5] The point here is that if the enterprise is worthwhile, the analogy of marriage seems particularly promising. It is an illustration of which Christian theologians have been somewhat chary, and the risks of naïvety, bad taste and out-and-out unwholesomeness in applying sexual imagery to the relationship between God and the soul are only too plain; but the dangers are perhaps at a minimum in the present context. The emphasis here is not on devotion nor on any kind of subjective feelings, but on the objective concept of unity-in-plurality, of two being united without losing their identities, of 'a union which does not destroy but fulfils', to use a phrase of Canon Allchin's which is exactly apt to my purpose.[6]

The greatest risk inherent in this personalist approach could be not anthropomorphism, not unwholesomeness, but proving too much. If we find it convincing we may overdo it and go on from it into idolatry or heresy. The concept of 'personal relationships' can be made into a touchstone in such a way that any relationship which claims to be a loving one is set up as holy and self-justifying.[7] On the contrary, we have to remember the ambivalence of the New Testament teaching about earthly affections. Nearest and dearest have to be given up, nothing grabbed can be kept, only what first dies can be resurrected. These are the terms of reference within which a Christian has to understand personal relationships. What he may say is not that they are self-justifying but that they are both demanding and enabling.

To think of them as *demanding* is to think of them as calling for a response. I should like to assert, with all caution, that in an important sense the proper response to relationship is *worship*, not only of God but of one another: taking worship to mean not uncritical or self-abasing adulation but the expression of reverent love. We might tentatively define it as 'the adequate response to holiness' and then go on

31

without idolatry to say that the finite holiness for which human beings are made is meant to call out a finite worship which is a true image for the infinite worship we owe to God.[8]

Likewise to call personal relationships *enabling* is to think of them as making possible what they demand, and so to speak of them in terms of *grace*, not only from God but also from one another. Marriage is a particularly good example of this, but to see the point we must leave *divine* grace completely out of account for the moment. Considering marriage simply humanly, as something which belongs to nature, we can recognize that *to this plain human reality*, taken apart from the Christian Gospel, categories of human grace apply, and not only apply but are integral to the understanding of what marriage means. This can be expressed by saying that there is a paradox in the concept of the 'duties of marriage'. If they are done as duties they are not truly done. Husbands and wives have a right to expect more of each other than their rights, and what is normal here is to transcend norms. A marriage into which no hint of such a possibility enters is not more but less natural than a marriage where more is given and taken than the plainly obligatory.[9]

Part of what the unity of marriage means is that the boundaries of self-interest are re-drawn, not just in ideal but in fact. So are the boundaries of individual capacity. Christians have been taught to say after St. Paul 'Not I, but Christ'. If they looked about them more they would recognize that the experience 'Not I, but the grace of my husband or wife' is at least as common. We build each other up in our human relationships, and are able to achieve by response what we could never manage by duty. So we can go on without idolatry to think of what we receive from one another in this way as a kind of human grace, a proper image for the grace of God.

This terminology of grace, unlike the terminology of worship, is not so much becoming archaic today as trivialized. We talk of doing something 'with a good grace', and might mean much more by it than we usually do. To do something truly 'with a good grace' is to find one's will responding to the will of another; and this to the theologically minded has a familiar ring. It is the doctrine of justification by faith. Contrariwise, there is a kind of 'justification by works' in the bad sense, prevalent in some human relationships including some marriages, as well as in people's relationships to God, where instead of 'bringing forth the fruit of the spirit' people try rather grimly to do what they ought in a spirit of self-sacrifice instead of unity.[10] 'What a good wife I am to do all the washing up on my own without complaining.' To see the difference between this and the 'justification by grace' which it misses might be to understand better both the theological virtue of faith and human fidelity. Fidelity does not notice it is making a sacrifice; or it is happy to admit a human need for help. It may be that we can learn as much about God's grace from the interplay of ordinary close human relationships, of dependence, independence, love, control and development, than from concentrating on theoretical divinity. If all goes well we shall not flatten out our concept of God but rather add a dimension to our conception of people.

This is the place to take up the sacramental theme by going on to ask whether these divine and human forms of worship have more in common still: whether these instances of grace have corresponding 'means of grace' by which they are characteristically expressed. The sacramental principle, we may say, is the idea that the inward and spiritual is properly and truly shown by the outward and visible. If a Christian considers seriously the teachings of his faith about creation and redemption he can find himself at home in the recognition that the universe is sacramental through and through: 'God saw that it was good', 'The Word was made flesh', 'This is my Body'. The prospect of a 'two-way illumination' between the divine and the human looks especially promising here, for one is led to consider the part played by physical bodies as expressive, for beings such as ourselves, of all that most matters to us. It is not irreverent, but of a piece with this sacramental understanding of the nature of the universe, to look on the physical act of sex in marriage as a human parallel to the religious sacraments, a human 'means of

33

grace' in which spiritual reality is truly mediated by material reality.[11]

This approach from the human side in no way disparages *divine* grace, recognized or even unrecognized. It is merely that the traditional religious understanding is being left on one side for the moment to let the human point stand out. So instead of hastening to say that marriage is 'a sacrament' we can describe it, almost literally, as a form of worship with its own sacrament.[12] To many Christians it is still important to go on to insist that marriage itself is a religious sacrament, but this doctrine is neither undermined nor established by the present argument.

The sacramental principle at its simplest is the assertion, as one might put it, that 'matter matters': that the physical is essentially the *vehicle* of the spiritual not an irrelevant or unsatisfactory appendage to it. Everything we do, we do through our bodies;[13] everything God does in the material world He does through material bodies. Our bodies are the way by which we express all our diverse relationships with other people, including our relationships with God. If this is comprehended the physical act of sex can be comprehended, not as a be-all and end-all nor as an unworthy distraction, but as the proper physical expression of that complete commitment of a man and a woman to each other which is marriage. Fornication then is seen as a cheapening and adultery as a betrayal of this human sacrament: both detach it from full commitment and set it up, as it were, as an idol in its own right.[14] Of course this moral judgment is an over-simplication: it is a sort of foundation, not a recipe, for Christian understanding of people and their problems.

In this context the characteristic *fertility* of marriage makes acceptable sense. It is sacramental not legalistic. There is no need to see offspring as an 'end of marriage' arbitrarily demanded from on high as a payment for the happiness human beings want for themselves. It is not misleading to emphasize instead that procreation is an analogy for creation and that here is one aspect of the image of God in mankind.[15] It is fair to claim as Christian and put together the two beliefs

34

that relationship is meant to be creative and that the spiritual is meant to be embodied in the physical. God Himself in Christian understanding is unity-in-plurality, and this fundamental relationship within God does not remain self-contained but gives life to derivative independent beings to delight their Creator and rejoice in one another. Human parenthood is constructively interpreted as a miniature model of this doctrine of God.[16]

It may be asked, which is the analogy, the human or the divine reality? The answer can surely be, Either, according to which way the world is being looked at. If we are trying to understand the unknown by the known, then the relationship between God and man is the unknown, to be approached with the help of the given fact, marriage. If we are trying to understand the copy from the original, then the human relationship can be interpreted as an image of the divine reality. It is maybe not without significance that when people refer from memory to the passage in the Epistle to the Ephesians[17] about the mystery of marriage as applied to Christ and the Church, they are often far from sure which is used there to illustrate which.

Another application can be made of the analogy between human and divine sacraments: not to stretch it too far, but to show it as adequate to some of the complexities of human existence. For both sorts of sacrament, there are those for whom they seem inappropriate. On the human side we have both bachelors and celibates; on the religious side there are certain sorts of Christians who for positive or negative reasons do not practice their faith sacramentally. There are those who find the physical 'means of grace' superfluous or alien, and those whose particular vocation it seems to be to abjure them. A sacramental theory which is obliged simply to repudiate the Quakers and to deprecate all those staunch Christians to whom non-sacramental worship is more real and natural than the Eucharist, is closing its eyes to facts. Of the importance of these 'believing but unsacramental men' Professor G. R. Dunstan has recently reminded us.[18] Maybe the Church could not live through the generations if most of its members were, so to speak, spiritual celibates or bachelors, but this need not mean that the proper place of these is to be denied. Of course the analogy is fanciful or even frivolous, but it might perhaps help some rather variegated Christians to understand one another.

For this analogical and personalist approach to prove satisfactory two basic requirements must be met. The first is that it must be broadly based if God is not to be belittled after all. No one human relationship, however illuminating, can be emphasized exclusively. There is a danger of proving too much: for instance, too great a reliance on the marriage analogy can lead one on, unnoticing, into seeming to say that the unmarried must be graceless. It is not just as marriage-able men and women that mankind is made in the image of the Trinity.[19] Likewise an emphasis on the characteristic creativeness of marriage might seem, hurtfully and unnecessarily, to make childless marriages something less than the real thing. Too great a reliance on any human analogy might lead one to forget that after all the relationship between God and man must be described partly by contrast and cannot be entirely swallowed up in likeness.[20] What is needed is a complex exploration of the various analogies available, father-child, king-subject, friend-friend, as well as husband-wife, not forgetting also the impersonal analogies such as light, a relating of these to each other and an alternation of analogy with contrast: remembering too that in all this we are illustrating possibilities not proving what we assert.

The second requirement is that whatever analogy is being used should indeed be based upon facts: that there should actually be these aspects of human relationships forcing themselves upon our attention whatever we want to say theologically. This implies that although we may hope, as I have indicated, for 'two-way illumination', we cannot use the argument to go both ways at once. We cannot say, for example, that because marriage is a striking image of the worship of God, we should therefore insist as a matter of social policy that marriages shall be exclusive. That would be a way to discredit both the Christian understanding of

36

marriage and the worship of God. It is only if we find as a matter of fact a bond between human beings which has this exclusive character not imposed upon it from outside but felt by those concerned to be intrinsic, that the theological analogy gets under way at all. Here again we have to insist that the problem of what to say about the failures and exceptions cannot be prejudged.

IV

SOCIAL REALITY

FROM what I have just been saying, marriage might appear to be an entirely private matter, and the Church's concern with it entirely the cure of individual souls. I have spoken of it in terms of personal relationships, which I have called demanding and enabling; and I have emphasized the concept of two becoming one, spiritually and physically. But now it needs to be emphasized in turn that a personal relationship is a complementary not a rival concept to a social institution. No relationship, however special, is an entirely private affair between the two people concerned. At the least it moulds them as social beings and makes its mark upon the way in which they face the world. Marriage in particular with its tendency to produce children becomes social not in spite of itself but characteristically. The community as such has a right to take an interest.

Of course in becoming a social institution a relationship is somewhat formalized; but this can be seen as stabilizing not as deadening. The people concerned do not cease to be individuals but they come to see themselves and be seen by others as fulfilling roles,[1] almost one might say as representatives rather than atomic units. The existentialist will scent 'bad faith' here, but I think he is profoundly wrong. Not many human beings are interesting enough to make much of life as unique individuals. If, for instance, to marry a man were only to offer him one's more distinctive traits one would also in effect be depriving him of those one lacked, as in decorating a room by choosing brick-red one eliminates pink. But it is also to become his *wife*, to take on this role, to draw upon, be supported by and hope to make available in this particular case whatever one has in common with the others of the

38

human race who have said in some form of words 'I take thee to my wedded husband'. Of course, people can lose themselves in their roles and abandon their proper individuality; and of course roles can shift or even disintegrate so that people fail to find support in them. Is 'working wife', for example, in any way the same role as 'obedient wife', once was? It is still worth pointing out that it is by the balancing and relating of the unique and the typical that most people can make some kind of sense of their lives in relationship with other people.

This does not contradict but supplements the argument of the last chapter. I described marriage as 'almost literally a form of worship', and forms of worship are not characteristically purely inward but have an inherent tendency to become institutionalized, to express themselves in social and ritual fashion. They are not, and do not normally seek to be, entirely free and private. This tendency can be overdone and become soul-destroying; or can become, in times of rapid change, a cause of controversy not a support; but ordinarily it is enriching to the individual to know himself part of something in which he can fulfil a role, not left to stand alone on his own feet to face reality.

It is therefore to be expected that much of what has been said about marriage can be developed in institutional terms, with a difference of emphasis but without contradiction. But if the Christian broadens out his understanding in this way he becomes vulnerable to the criticism of the world. Has he maybe got his picture of the kind of social reality marriage is all wrong? Here the real criticisms of the Christian view begin and need to be responsibly met. An English Christian, particularly if he is happily married, will tend to assume that what he wants to say about relationships in marriage and what his whole upbringing has taught him to say about marriage as an institution are two sides of one coin and that this coin ought to be legal tender for everyone; but these assumptions are far from self-evident. Even granted that this accepting attitude is possible and natural, it is hardly inevitable. Still less can it guarantee any particular institutional form as the only proper mould into which to pour the molten metal of human relationships.

This whole discussion is being conducted against a background of revolt against institutions in general, and of more specific discontent with the peculiar strictness with which the Christian Church regards the institution of marriage. Far from being disposed to accept the Church's particular teaching on divorce, the world is casting doubt on marriage itself, the norm to which divorce is the exception. The Church, rightly, does not ignore this discontent. It tries to answer it by arguments about human needs and human happiness; but once having appealed to the facts, to the facts it must go. If the Christian view of marriage turns out not to answer to the experienced realities of the world, then on the face of it there is something wrong with the Christian view of marriage. Worse, the understanding of marriage is sufficiently central to the understanding of human nature to put at risk here the whole Christian doctrine of man and therefore the whole of Christian theology. So great is the relevance of the present discontents, in so far as they are founded upon genuine human experience and not to be dismissed as merely irresponsible heresy.

The temptation for both sides is to proceed by way of affirmation and counter-affirmation. 'Man needs stable monogamy for his true fulfilment in marriage.' 'Man needs to break free from the shackles of ecclesiastical authority and find for himself what is good.' It is worth remembering that *neither* of these statements is self-supporting: because our own is not, it does not follow that the contrasting one is, either. The way to proceed cannot be by facile dogmatism nor by an equally facile assumption that what is unpalatable to us must be true.

My own predilection here is to flout philosophical warnings and to try, with all diffidence, to get an 'ought' from an 'is'.[2] It does not seem unreasonable to consider in the light of all the information we can muster what human nature truly is and so what kinds of institutions are suitable to it. This is a 'natural law' approach, in what would like to be modern dress. On the face of it, there *is* a good deal to be said for stable monogamous unions where they can be achieved. They have a sort of basic suitability for the way the world is. If instead it had been the case, for instance, that the numbers of men and women were grossly uneven; that constancy to one person could be shown to have damaging consequences; that only the highly intelligent were capable of understanding the meaning of fidelity; that physical beauty had an irresistible effect; or that children flourished better removed from their own parents: then marriage as the institution we know would be unjustifiable. It is admittedly totally impossible to free oneself from prejudice here. Probably the best one can do is to become aware of what one's prejudices are, and not to pretend to be surprised when the right rabbit comes out of the hat of human nature. To put it in more dignified terms, it is more realistic to attempt to give reasons for the faith that is in one than to suppose that one can start like Descartes from nothing and arrive at something.

To make such a 'natural law' approach even clear, let alone convincing, it is needful to show at which point it is based on theology. Part of the reasons why natural law has such a bad name in some quarters is not just that it gets 'ought' from 'is', but that the 'is' from which it derives its 'ought' is a collection of more or less arbitrary divine fiats handed down by the Church without regard for human circumstances. On the contrary, natural law may be much more constructively understood as a system which does admittedly get 'ought' from 'is', but not from inhuman commands, but from the 'is' of human nature. Theology comes in, not to promulgate laws, but to give its account of what human nature is: to the Christians, created, fallen and redeemed nature.

The charge this kind of natural law view has to face is not arbitrariness but circularity. At the outset, it may be said, by describing mankind in this way it begs the question of what human nature requires, and so it is hardly surprising that a Christian ethic comes out of the hat. So, as usual, one will in the end be thrown back upon apologetic, to show cause

41

why one understands human nature in this way to start with. This is no objection: it would ill become a Christian to be afraid for his faith to be investigated. If no Christians are prepared to show why they believe that human beings are God's creatures, that they are fallen creatures, and that God has redeemed them, then the Christian faith will not be found on the earth.

Any Christian view of marriage must depend on the convincingness of the Christian faith; but that convincingness it may itself help or hinder. For many people the Church's past and indeed present attitude towards humanity's sexual nature is a real stumbling block to Christianity as such. Unfortunately there is much to be deplored. Mankind's fallen condition is only too easy to believe in and only too easy to illustrate from our religious history. There is no knockdown case either way: we cannot expect to be able to say tidily that the Church has been right or wrong about sex. The truth is as usual a matter of fair balancing of emphases. It is likely to be best served not by attacks on sin nor attacks on bigotry but by the setting out of a positive view to see if it can stand up. That is what this relational account of marriage as a human institution is aiming at.

This is no place for a massive historical or sociological survey; there is no need for example to try to summarize or rewrite Dr. Sherwin Bailey's great book *The Man-Woman Relation in Christian Thought*. What is needed though if a Christian view of marriage is to be maintained today is a willingness to reckon with what can be said against it. For a Christian the divorce problem looms large because it is a question within the Church where a definitely Christian line has to be taken and may go wrong. But for the problem of divorce to arise at all a norm of marriage has to be presupposed, and today this norm itself is coming under explicit attack. It is being responsibly asserted that marriage as Christians have understood it is not so attractive, even as an ideal, as they have supposed. Before continuing to discuss the norm in Christian terms and considering whether it can have any exceptions it is advisable to look briefly at two of the main objections which are being brought against it, not to answer them exhaustively but to show that they are not being ignored. The Christian attitude towards sex is supposed to be discredited because it debases the role of woman; and to be now out of date because of the discovery of effective contraception which has made the permissive society an attainable rival ideal. A would-be Christian account of marriage should at least sketch an answer to each of these.

It is true that in most times and places men have been the dominant sex, often to the detriment of women; but it is a nice historical question whether Christianity has characteristically supported or undermined this tendency. As so often, diverse claims can be made in Christ's name. 'In Christ there is no male or female.' 'The husband is the head of the wife, as Christ also is the head of the Church.' Christ himself made friends of women, his followers, from whom we have all our knowledge of him, continued to keep them firmly in their place. Both these strands have been strong in the subsequent centuries and they will not be unravelled by polemic.

Unfortunately polemic is always tempting to Christians as well as to those who disagree with them. There is the straightforward kind which evades the unpleasant facts and scores over an adversary. There is the more insidious back-handed kind which tries to disarm the adversary by disowning the views or conduct of fellow Christians, whether of this or another century, in the name of enlightenment. When St. Paul and St. Augustine for example are smoothly made into the villains of the story it is time to remember that they are members of the communion of saints, claiming not reverence so much as courtesy when their outlook and the outlook of their times is opaque to us, and particularly when we think they went wrong. The preacher who is supposed to have said 'St. Paul says and I do in part agree' was maybe not on such wrong lines as if he had said, 'Of course, St. Paul was anti-woman'.

It is no more necessary for a would-be Christian to be able to defend the Church in detail down the ages than for him

43

to relish the attack upon it. What matters for a Christian view of marriage to be tenable is not that human life should always have been understood in ways congenial to the twentieth century but that what Christians assert should be capable of making lasting sense of God's purposes for mankind. We have no right to talk about *God's* purposes unless the links with our religious tradition are plain; but we have come to see that we have no right to talk about God's purposes for *mankind* if our doctrine is not compatible with a wholehearted appreciation of women as human beings. For such an appreciation I believe it is more constructive to stress complementarity rather than either subordination or equality.

If one is no sociologist the temptation is to generalize, even dogmatically, from one's own situation. Happy people stress the joys and privileges of their condition; the unfortunate stress the injustice and precariousness of their lot; and both can be right. Set both to read the account of the good wife in the last chapter of the Book of Proverbs, and the reactions are likely to be diverse. The 'Mothers' Union' stereotype will glory in the scope offered to the 'virtuous woman': 'she considereth a field, and buyeth it. . . . She perceiveth that her merchandise is profitable'; and still more in the warmth of relations in which she will live. 'The heart of her husband trusteth in her. . . . Her children rise up, and call her blessed.' The 'Women's Lib.' stereotype will point out that all this is by favour of her husband, not by right. He sets a price on her, though it be 'above rubies'. It is up to him to 'give her of the fruit of her hands' and it is he who is 'known in the gates, when he sitteth among the elders of the land'.

Both sides in this question have something unpalatable to accept. On the one hand the contented ones ought to realize that the stridency of 'Women's Lib.' is rooted in an unhappiness deep enough to be called misery among some women *as* women. Misery will not yield to preaching. It is not much use to point out that housekeeping can be a complex, dignified and satisfying role to those who have already failed to find it so. It is still less use to point out that a married woman has

44

taken on a certain job and has no right to jib at its conditions, that all jobs have their drudgery and that she chose it with open eyes. It may too easily be replied that truly satisfying jobs do not need all this defending; that the loneliness, fatigue and diminishment that some women find in child-minding and housework are not fully predictable in advance; and above all that many women have little choice in 'taking on this job' if they want the satisfactions of family life, whereas men choose their occupations and have family life as well. It is right for happy people who have no need to be strident to do justice to these arguments.

The unpalatable fact which any feminist has to face is that there really is no complete answer to all this. Changing the system would not solve all the problems unless biology could be changed as well. Women have the babies, and indeed they generally want to have the babies. They are physically capable of bearing them and as a rule psychologically capable of bearing with them; and the former is not a matter of conditioning even if the latter is. There is this 'homekeeping' role which has developed over the centuries and there are plenty of reasons why it will not simply go away. Many women are wholly and many more partially content with it. It can and should be adjusted, maybe in some respects radically, but it can hardly be abolished. There is plenty of scope for policies of encouragement and especially for the breaking down of isolation. Unstinted part-time work, more playgroups (good for child and for mother), less segregation of generations out of each other's reach, all seem worth striving for; but none of these will make women's lives indistinguishable from men's.

What can a Christian say about the position of women in the light of all this? This is where 'complementarity' can come in, though this could easily become as patronising and stultifying as subordination. 'Separate but equal' is not a phrase with a happy history. The only hope is to get away from rights altogether and to think rather in terms of what human beings can happily do for one another. Then maybe the *domestic* aspects of women's role can become less pre-

45

eminent and the stress can be put instead on *relationship* as a deep human need which women are characteristically able to foster. For this there is both modern evidence and ancient authority. For instance, questions of personal relationships are typical 'women's page subjects'; and woman is created in the Book of Genesis not as housekeeper but as companion. The standard wifely and motherly roles can arise naturally out of this primary one in a way which is much less easily seen in reverse. On the other hand, revolts large or small against domesticity, or different apportionments of daily tasks between men and women, need not on this view necessarily be seen as revolts against womanliness. Instead of saying sweepingly 'Woman's place is in the home', we can say cautiously 'Woman's characteristic vocation is in relationship', and add if we wish that home is a place where relationships are apt to be built. So we could learn to allow better for the contents and discontents of different women.

Biology, I have assumed, cannot be changed: but nowadays in a way it can, at least to the extent that women can choose whether or not to have children without forgoing sex. At last the old 'double standard' of morality for men and women can be abolished; but in a direction uncomfortable for Christians. The serious question arises whether Christian marriage, necessary for so long as a protection for children, is now out of date. A Christian will never understand 'the permissive society' if he sees it simply as a repudiation of morality. It purports to be a change of morality, based on a change of facts. Once, it can plainly be said, sex outside marriage was indeed wrong because it led sooner or later to unwanted children; now all that is changed and since there is nothing wrong with sex as such it is quite responsible for people to have impermanent relationships so long as they know what they are doing. This is the case the Christian has to answer.

Even if he thinks that the medical desirability of longterm contraception is not yet secure, he had best assume it for the sake of the argument, or he will commit himself to changing his mind about chastity when medical science is only a little more advanced than it is now. If he still believes

46

that chastity is and remains right for its own sake it is important to consider why he thinks so. For many Christians the New Testament unanimity is the decisive argument; but its application to the new conditions of the twentieth century cannot be automatic. What is needed is not an appeal to authority but a rationale for traditional chastity as still worth while. If this rationale turns out still to be partly an appeal to prudence it need not be the worse for that. On the contrary, nothing but an appeal to prudence will fully counter the current argument that permissiveness is better for us than chastity. Arguments for the moral beauty of chastity may have great appeal in particular cases but no general force.

Arguments for purity are ineffective when on the one hand traditionalists no longer want to suggest that sex itself is impure while on the other hand nobody is advocating promiscuity. The real defence of chastity which is independent of medical developments, though not independent of the facts of human nature, is the praise of fidelity.[3] Fidelity is not easily praised, except in its rare heroic forms. There is something immodest about dragging its quieter manifestations out into the open: immodest in the sense of 'unseemly', and often in the sense of 'conceited' as well. Yet it needs to be said that the kind of semi-permanent commitments which are being seriously recommended today, however they may overcome the various sorts of speedy retribution which have traditionally beset 'sin', still have an abiding and intrinsic risk. They could lose by default an immensely valuable form of human happiness, the fundamental trust which can develop when marriage is fully monogamous. This possibility of happiness is worth protection lest it should disappear before it is even missed.

At the moment, in reaction against the shallowness of 'they lived happily ever after', young people are being implicitly taught that the time for happiness is now. Curiously enough, traditionalist teaching is also capable of going this way. Its message is sometimes 'You mustn't just grab the happiness you have now: you must pay for it later in lasting fidelity'; and already this is unhappily defeatist. It unconsciously creates a picture of middle age as a time when romance will have faded and when all that remains will be 'compensations' which accrue, quite legalistically, to the conventionally moral. This is a long way from the gospel of giving and receiving, of 'good measure, pressed down, shaken together and running over', if only we go with the grain of the universe and not against it. One's wedding day ought not to be the happiest day of one's life. It would be truer as well as more inviting to speak of fidelity to people getting married not as if it were a tax to be paid but as a development of the present happiness which is only just beginning.[4] In this way we can commend a virtue rather than condemn a vice.

There is no need to be hasty in passing judgment on people who have missed this happiness, even if they have missed it apparently through their own fault. The aim is to make this happiness possible, not to knock down those who in Christian eyes have failed. In this context premarital unchastity can be seen by Christians as a grave error. It does not have to be either a specially wicked sin or perfectly all right. It is hard to forgive in the way that all sins against prudence, great or small, are hard to forgive, because it is hard to undo. When unchastity is more than this, it is when it is a sin against a particular person's love; and for a Christian who knows what he is about that person may be God. Such a sin could still be 'deadly', but it is not for other Christians even to judge between husband and wife, still less to try to pass judgment on God's behalf, only to try to understand what chastity is for and how it is right for human beings.

So Christians still have the right and duty to set up stable monogamous marriage and commend it to the world as more than an ideal, as a proper *norm* for human beings.[5] But still they must be careful not to over-reach themselves. A norm is not the same thing as an invariable law, and the attempt to make it so can be as cruel as the failure to defend it. On the contrary, to call marriage a norm has another implication, welcome or unwelcome, that exceptions are not unthinkable. In a way this consequence must be called welcome, not because divorce is in any way desirable but because it

48

happens. What is welcome is to be able to allow for this fact without having to make divorce as 'normal' as marriage. Instead we can say that a strong norm ought to be capable of 'carrying' some exceptions without itself being materially weakened.

It is certain that this particular norm has always had exceptions to carry. Divorce is not a new problem for our age, nor is it really part of the 'permissive society'. It is the much older question of *how* stable marriage has to be to work as a norm at all. Christians want to go beyond 'stable' to 'indissoluble', and therefore they must keep on asking whether the setting up of this norm which is supposed to be for our good is actually exacting too high a toll in human misery from those who are unequal to it. Part of their answer will be their defence of the norm itself as a worthy idea; but part of it ought to be a readiness to show mercy both practically and theoretically to those who are not able to conform to it. It ill becomes a Christian, especially a happily married Christian, to offer up his fellow human beings as living sacrifices on the altar of 'Christian marriage'. If the valued 'indissolubility' of his own marriage demands this, is it not a false god?

On the contrary, if 'indissolubility' means anything it is something real and identifiable which stands up without artificial props. It is a slogan for what marriage can be like, which people can make their *own* by finding that they have lived their way into it, not something to force upon others for whom the idea may be at best empty and at worst bitterly cruel. That is, it is to be looked for where it is, not where it is not; but *where* it is, it is no chimaera. What it signifies is not a sort of trap in which one is caught but a strong unshakable floor to stand on. When married people find themselves standing on such a floor they have the right to say, 'This, not pettiness, inadequacy and turmoil, is the reality of marriage, the practical vindication of the teaching. It can happen and is worth commending.'

D

V

INDISSOLUBLE BOND

IT may sound agreeable to common sense and even to Christian charity to talk about marriage as a human norm and maybe a norm with exceptions; but Christian theology has also a great deal to say about marriage which has often been incompatible with this way of thinking. Whatever marriage is for the world, it has been believed that there is besides something called 'Christian marriage', established by the Lord, which is absolutely unbreakable in this life. It is high time to try and reckon with this ancient and authoritative but not undisputed teaching.

Any Christian thinker trying to reach understanding has three sets of data: the Bible, the tradition of the Church, and current experience. The interpretation of each of these requires experts, and if one is no expert one must do the best one can with the help of those who are. Of the three kinds, the first and the last are fundamental: to ignore the Bible is to stop speaking as a Christian and to ignore experience is to lose the right to pronounce about anything, including Christianity. To ignore tradition is to saw off the branch one is sitting on, but still in a way tradition may be regarded as less 'hard' data than the other two. If it is not dead it is still in the moulding and one is even part of the way it is being moulded now. To repudiate it extensively would be presumptuous but not self-contradictory. From all these data there has emerged in the course of generations the Christian idea of the *vinculum*, the indissoluble bond of marriage.

This bond has often been described as something 'metaphysical' over and above the plain facts of experience. I must admit before starting to argue about it that such a notion is bound to be uncongenial if one has been trained in empiricist philosophy and taught to mistrust metaphysics: it is necessary to make an effort to be fair to it. The undoubted attraction of the 'indissoluble' side in the divorce question is not, I believe, that marriage vows as such necessarily set up a mysterious bond, but that Christ taught that divorce is against God's will, and this was no vague ideal but a truly 'hard saying'. On this basis the Church, like Moses, may have to recognize the validity of divorce for the world but must have great heart-searchings before it can have any part or lot in it. We must come back to these heart-searchings later;[1] but if this turns out to be a proper approach, 'metaphysical' indissolubility becomes much less relevant, and it is difficult to argue convincingly against a notion which one is tempted to reject out of hand as meaningless. Yet there are many who do not wish so to reject it. When a notion patently has plenty of life in it something must be done to face it, and to face it as defended by its best not its worst exponents.

Mr. John Lucas for example[2] has impressively based his case for the traditional unbreakable bond not on abstract metaphysics but on the reality of human actions and the need to grasp the fact that though the past can be redeemed it can never be altered. So marriage vows set up an entity which is there for evermore whatever those concerned subsequently come to feel about it. This argument is a good corrective to the woolly-mindedness of those who are concerned only that everyone should be happy in the short run: but the trouble is that it tries to prove too much.

When a man and woman take each other as man and wife (not, incidentally, when they vow eternal constancy) they bring into being a marriage. It is truly said that nothing can ever alter the fact that this has happened; but it still remains to enquire what this entity is which has come to exist, and one may still have to ask whether it is totally indestructible. To affirm that it does now exist and therefore will always *have* existed does not prove that it always *will* exist. The Church has always taught that death can destroy it; on what grounds is it so certain that nothing but death can?

Mr. Lucas acknowledges[3] that some relationships are impermanent; but he affirms 'not so with marriage', and goes

51

on to state the Christian view in its strictest form. It would be for a biblical critic to show authoritatively that he has made too big a jump here.[4] But the weighing of data cannot be left entirely to experts, and every Christian must somehow twist the three strands of Bible, tradition and experience into a rope on to which he can hold. What I want to suggest is that the question, 'Is marriage indissoluble or is it dissoluble?' may be a little like 'Have you stopped beating your mother?' To a Christian it is monstrous to say that marriage is 'dissoluble', but instead of taking refuge in the theory of a metaphysical bond to which earthly facts can make no difference, he would be wise to consider that the truth may be more complex.

If one looks at the biblical data again with as little prejudice as possible three facts seem to emerge with some clarity. First, that Christ taught that divorce is contrary to God's will. Secondly, that his teaching has a sternness and urgency which ought to forbid attempts to water it down in his name. Thirdly, that his teaching had a freedom from legalistic categories and a sovereign mercy for sinners which should equally forbid attempts to apply it mechanically or meanly. On the one hand we have the saying 'He who putteth away his wife and marrieth another, committeth adultery against her';[5] on the other hand we have a vast amount of illustration of the unpredictable ways in which God deals with people; these balanced against each other seem to make both liberal 'dissolubility' and rigorist 'indissolubility' alike unpromising ways of understanding what marriage truly is.

In a parallel way the data of experience exhibit both the point and the difficulty of talking about the marriage bond as unbreakable. On the one hand it is worth emphasizing, especially in the midst of an argument which casts doubt on the idea of a *metaphysical* bond, that 'indissolubility' can be found *in* experience. It is not only possible but ordinary for the lives of a man and a woman to be so joined that they constitute a unity, which there is simply no question of 'putting asunder'. The biblical expression 'one flesh' is not theoretical but answers to something in human life.

On the other hand, experience has a destructive effect upon a rigorist interpretation of what 'indissolubility' means. It has always been necessary for legislators, for the hardness of people's hearts, to allow them sometimes to put away their wives. A rigorist ought to hold that all this from the Mosaic law onwards has been no more than a licensing of adultery. The fact that rigorists are generally no more able than liberals to believe this when confronted with real human beings is a stronger argument against the rigorist interpretation of 'indissolubility' than the sort of argument from compassion which can be called sentimental. If marriage is a metaphysical bond which persists whatever happens then all those who go through wedding ceremonies with people who have had divorces are and continue to be adulterers for whom repentance must mean giving up their sin. If in its rigour this cannot be held in Christ's name, it behoves those who are inclined to believe in 'indissolubility' of any kind to have a searching look at what they mean by it.

It is from the third strand, tradition, that the idea that the indissolubility of marriage is something supernatural comes. This was not arbitrarily invented by the Church but is supposed to follow logically and necessarily from the New Testament teaching. In particular there is the passage in the Epistle to the Ephesians,[6] justly prized by those who believe that Christianity is far from being anti-sex, which describes marriage as a 'great mystery' because it signifies the union of Christ and his Church. How could such a bond be dissolved without blasphemy? Dr. Sherwin Bailey in tracing the history of the theory has explained clearly what it has amounted to. For this way of thinking, Christian marriages have not only been an illustration of Christ's perpetual marriage with the Church, 'but also partook of its very character; . . . they acquired immediately and for ever the inviolability of their supernatural antitype'.[7]

The building of this elaborate superstructure has unfortunately sometimes concealed its real foundation, but this is still there underneath. It remains true that the most obvious interpretation of Christ's teaching on marriage is indissolubility of some sort. What the theory completely loses sight of is the fact that the most obvious interpretation of some aspects of human life is dissolubility of some sort.

The question which any onesided view evades is whether it is possible to do justice to both, and at the same time to the converse data of the mercy in Christ's teaching and the possibility of indissolubility in experience. The recent tradition of the Church of England confronted with all this has been to affirm the *fact* of indissolubility with increasing conviction while avoiding the *word*,[8] thereby rendering further investigation both desirable and possible.

Meanwhile the philosophical climate, though appreciably kinder to metaphysical systems than it was some years ago, is still hostile to statements about supposed facts which nothing in experience can touch. The trouble with metaphysical assertions of this kind is 'that it is unclear what would count for or against them, establish or refute them'.[9] Worse, in some cases it is clear that nothing is going to be allowed to count against them, that they are to be upheld in the teeth of experience, against any empirical evidence. It may surely be reckoned a solid philosophical gain that the onus is now on those who want to make such assertions to show that they have any real meaning.

To many people the statement that a marriage, whatever happens to it, is still in existence is just such a useless metaphysical assertion. The trouble is not exactly that it is an *empty* statement. Indeed if it were merely empty its exponents might be allowed to go on talking harmless highsounding nonsense if they wanted to. But in this case all manner of practical consequences are drawn about the wrongness of attempted divorce and remarriage. What makes the theory open to attack by any philosopher who has learnt from the anti-metaphysicians is not, in this case, that it means *nothing*, but that it is supposed to be *impregnable*, to be true whatever happens. If nothing is to be allowed to count against it, its meaning is of a strangely inaccessible kind. When the theory turns out to have unacceptable practical consequences, philosophical discontent is backed up by moral discontent

54

and a strong suspicion builds up that the fully fledged traditional doctrine of indissoluble marriage is a human not a divine deliverance.

Even such an authoritative and sensitive exposition as that of Professor Schillebeeckx of the doctrine that 'the basis of absolute indissolubility is . . . to be found in Christian baptism',[10] lends itself readily to caricature when one tries to see what it amounts to. One is tempted to envisage baptism as a kind of chemical which has the property of making the glue of marriage if applied later set absolutely hard. If in a sounder appreciation of the loyalty and intellectual power which down the generations have gone into the attempt to follow out logically the New Testament teaching, one still feels that something has gone wrong, one may be seized by a less irreverent comparison.

Like the doctrine of the metaphysical *vinculum* in marriage, the doctrine of transubstantiation of the elements in the Eucharist has taken its rise in a strenuous attempt to interpret the New Testament data with integrity. 'They shall be one flesh': 'This is my body': is it not natural to suppose that in each case at a given moment something mysterious, maybe miraculous, is to happen, after which whatever the outward facts may look like the true nature of things is permanently altered? Yet in each case the resulting emphasis on a solemn formula, to which both God and man are to be held, whose function is to create super-sensible entitles, has led the Church into bitter and unconstructive controversies. In each case the unpalatable character to many people of the practical consequences and the *built-in* irrefutability of the theory has led to impatient rejection of its whole intent. The Eucharist is reduced to a mere memorial service, marriage to a dissoluble contract.

As long as the argument continues in these terms of reference nothing but deadlock and prejudice comes of it. Yet in the case of the Eucharist the whole picture has recently changed, and somehow Christians on both sides of the argument have found themselves able to approach again the concept of Real Presence, of the Lord giving himself to his people as he promised in the breaking of the bread, which the controversy has tended to obscure for everyone.[11]

What could be the equivalent for marriage doctrine of the recovery of Real Presence for Eucharistic doctrine? There is an attractive account by Professor Macquarrie of the nature of the marriage bond,[12] which ought to take us some way forward. He prefers the term 'ontological' which means to do with the essence of things and stresses the *real* character of the bond, rather than 'metaphysical' which stresses its 'beyondness'. In giving a place to real human commitment in the midst of our increasingly 'throwaway' society;[13] in emphasizing that the marriage bond is made of several strands consolidated over the years rather than springing almost magically into being on the pronouncing of certain words; above all by understanding the bond as essentially personal: Professor Macquarrie has convincingly said what needs saying about the indissolubility of marriage. Nor has he taken 'Christian marriage' apart as something wholly distinct from human marriage in the sight of God.

He does not repudiate the term 'metaphysical' but his understanding of what it means for the marriage bond is a long way from the realm of mysterious untestable entities legalistically conceived which the idea of a 'metaphysical *vinculum*' conjures up in many people's minds. Instead one is in the region of the personal and moral, where 'metaphysical' suggests aspects of reality over and above what we can see and touch, but not completely out of reach: something 'more' in I. T. Ramsey's phrase, which is capable of being 'disclosed', not something we are bound to believe in but can never get hold of. There is no need after all for a metaphysical bond to be something sinister. It need be no more than a real moral bond, provided that morality itself is understood in a sufficiently metaphysical way, as something beyond ourselves which we do not make but find to be binding upon us. It is this objectivity, this reality, which the word 'ontological' is brought in to emphasize.

It must then seem at least ungrateful and maybe tendentious to disagree eventually with Professor Macquarrie's essential point that the reality of the marriage bond proves its indissolubility in the strictest sense. It still appears necessary to point out obstinately that a real bond is not thereby proved to be an indissoluble bond. 'Dissoluble' after all is a metaphor: marriage will not melt like ice, but perhaps it might melt like gold?

Professor Macquarrie takes his stand with Professor Schillebeeckx who has distinguished two different historic views of indissolubility only to unite them again.[14] It seems clear that the Fathers and particularly Augustine taught that marriage *ought* not to be dissolved, and that it was the scholastics who came to insist that it *could* not be dissolved. Professor Schillebeeckx proceeds to fit these together,[15] and one can see how this makes sense: if marriage ought not to be dissolved, if its moral rights and duties are 'valid for life', then for anyone who cares about morality as a Christian must care, marriage *cannot* be dissolved. Is it so clear though that the resulting doctrine is the only one possible for a loyal Christian? Some Christians will still want to argue that 'ought not' and 'cannot' are distinct ideas which conflict rather than implying one another.[16] To say that people literally cannot have divorces abolishes the real sin of putting asunder what God has joined. This sin cannot be properly recognized by those who have to say that a broken marriage has not been put asunder at all, because either it is still in being or else it never existed.

According to Bishop Butler's useful tautology 'everything is what it is and not another thing'. The present suggestion is that a broken marriage is a broken marriage; something that stands out as an unnatural smashing of what was built to last, a blasphemy against the unity of Christ and his Church, an amputation inflicted upon a living body: not a figment of the imagination, a chimaera, a squared circle. The bond of marriage is indeed a real bond, affecting those who are joined in it for evermore. It can never be neatly untied, only harshly severed. When this injury has happened the practical question is how the wound can best be healed, and the temptation is always either to cover it soothingly up at grave risk of its

57

festering, or to keep it open for ever as a warning to others. It needs to be said that if it turns out that even grave injuries can sometimes be healed, there is no question of saying that they were not injuries, of 'changing the norm'.[17] The norm is the healthy, the indestructible marriage which can properly be called indissoluble because its permanence is just not open to question. It may be that its real indissolubility can be the better appreciated because it is not deemed to be indissoluble apart from the facts.[18]

This, I believe, is the view of the marriage bond which does most justice to all the data: that marriage is properly and characteristically indissoluble, that to dissolve it is always an aberration. One could borrow a legal term here and say that the indissolubility of marriage could be a *defeasible* concept.[19] Or one could express the idea more theologically by saying that 'they shall be one flesh' is as normal and human as 'thou shalt love the Lord thy God', but perhaps no more automatic. This 'hard saying' would be an impossibly hard saying apart from grace, which is not to say that only Christian marriages have a hope of success, but that marriage is one of the places in human life where grace most characteristically operates through human beings. The hard sayings of Christ are not difficult to keep: they are either totally impossible or natural fruits of the spirit.[20] The matter has been precisely put by Professor Dunstan [21]: 'The great word of *Genesis*, that a man shall cleave unto his wife, and they shall become one flesh . . . is at once command and promise. It is a command: press on to that unity, for the sake of your perfection; see that you fall not out by the way; do not give up, do not forsake the covenant yourself; and if the other does, remember God in Christ, faithful to his bride, the Church, and so forgive, to the uttermost. This is the command of God. And the promise is that this, the impossible, is possible. The two do become one, and "signify", or exemplify to the world, "the mystical union that is betwixt Christ and his Church". What God commands he also gives.'

For the Church to put this doctrine of marriage into practice in dealing with individuals is anything but straightforward.

Many Christians will think it far less trouble to hold on to the simplest doctrine of indissolubility in spite of all that can be said against it. They will point out with some justice that this more difficult view of a real norm which humanly speaking admits of exceptions is in practice very perilous, for exceptions always tend to spread and devour the norm. This fact will always have to be taken into account by anyone who hopes to put the present view into practical effect, or the results will be indistinguishable from plain dissolubility. The concern of the argument so far has been to show that at least a theoretical distinction can be made: to set out the idea of an indissoluble bond which is *characteristic* of marriage, as different both from a bond which is indissoluble by definition and from a bond which can simply be dissolved.

This is not just to say pointlessly that marriage is indissoluble when it is indissoluble, but rather that we have not fully understood what marriage means unless we have understood that two people can be so joined that divorce is unthinkable. Likewise, we have not understood the meaning of the word 'human' unless we have grasped the possibility of a reasoning and loving being: but some people are unreasonable and unloving, and beyond a certain point we call them 'inhuman'. Just so marriages are characteristically indissoluble, but some fail, and beyond a certain point we have to call them 'dissoluble'. To do so need not be to impugn the good ones; it is to ask that they shall be allowed to 'carry' the exceptions,[22] neither ignoring them nor making them the norm.

VI

HARVEST OF THE SPIRIT

I HAVE suggested that the question, 'Is marriage dissoluble or indissoluble?' may be misconceived, a little like the question, 'Have you stopped beating your mother?' It has too much packed up in it. A closer parallel will make the point more clearly. The question about whether marriage is dissoluble really is like the question, 'Is your right hand expendable?' 'Of course not' is the proper, instant answer: my right hand is as much needed, and as much my own, as anything I have; but it remains true that people have had, and survived, amputations. I should be foolish to live my life in a state of readiness for such a wretched contingency, imagining every cut finger turning to blood poisoning, finding out about artificial limbs, adjusting myself to the idea. But if it came to that, then I should have to do the best I could, and other people would have to do what they could to help, even if the loss had been my own fault. The comparison emphasizes the normal, not just ideal, indissolubility of marriage, and conversely the emergency character of divorce, its hurt and distress. It can help us not to slide into the premature assumption that we have a 'permissive society' in which divorce is a reasonable voluntary upheaval like moving house, maybe exhausting, maybe saddening, maybe forced by circumstances, but potentially something people want and choose to do.

That is all very well, it may be sternly replied, but what has become of the teaching of Christ? Does this comparison of divorce with amputation forsake the clear Christian message that divorce is not just unpleasant but forbidden? It is fair to insist that to speak of divorce as a cutting off of part of oneself is no newfangled unbiblical notion. On the contrary, it is a way of expounding the biblical image that man and wife are 'one flesh'. But still it must be admitted that it does nothing at all to explain 'whosoever shall put away his wife, and marry another, committeth adultery against her'.[1] This is the hardest saying on marriage, the one that makes every theory except rigorism look like an evasion. I have preferred the positive statement, the quotation from Genesis, that a man shall 'leave his father and mother, and cleave to his wife . . . so then they are no more twain, but one flesh', as a foundation for a Christian doctrine of marriage,[2] but it is no use to have a favourite text and brush aside the rest with a glib reminder that we do not have Christ's actual words. It is of course not actual words which are in question but the whole spirit of our tradition. If we are not to be totally agnostic, we know that Christ said something difficult and, it seems, unpalatable about divorce: like the famous preacher on sin, he was 'against it'. We have to keep asking in the light of this conviction where our loyalty lies today.

Rigorism is not lightly to be done away with. The fact that there are hard cases does not in itself disprove it, and nor does the fact that there are all sorts of ingenious ways of explaining away what Christ is supposed to have said prove liberalism. The parts of Christianity one wants to reject could be the parts one needs; and just because one knows one is not being selfish, it does not follow that one is not being weak. What impugns rigorism is not that its consequences are hard but that sometimes they are nonsense,[3] and nonsense in terms of the very teaching of Christ to which they seek to be loyal. If it has to be assumed that there is no such thing as divorce, then people who find out what married life can be in a stable second union, after one of them has made a disastrous early mistake, are as much 'living in sin' as people who take lovers; whereas someone who espouses a divorced woman, gets tired of her, is divorced and remarries, is not living in sin at all. These are not obscure outside cases: they are the kind of thing which really happens; and if the Church is to adopt a rigorist stance it can have nothing to say to them. A rigorist can have no advice whatever to offer to people who have thoroughly committed themselves a second time but who want after all to be real Christians. He can have no constructive

61

advice to offer to those divorced people who lacking any vocation to celibacy find themselves unable to manage on their own. Sometimes such people are exhorted to 'live single' by God's grace, when 'single' is precisely what they are supposed not to be. Surely in all this Christians are coming under the judgment of Christ, 'They bind heavy burdens and grievous to be borne, and lay them on men's shoulders . . . '.[4]

In the light of all this we need, not just want, an interpretation of Christ's teaching which avoids rigorism. It must not be a fine-spun learned interpretation, but an understanding which can make sense to any believer simple or sophisticated. It seems reasonable to have a look at the Sermon on the Mount: that presentation of Christ's teaching as the new law more absolute than the old. Here we find one form of that comparison of divorce with adultery which is the cause of our perplexity; but it does not stand alone. It is set in a context of alarming comparisons: a lustful glance is also adultery; anger is on a footing with murder; defence of one's belongings is selfish. To be rigorist about any of these would be ludicrous, and most people manage only too easily to be liberal about these claims or oblivious of them. They are looked on generally as optional extras, 'counsels of perfection' indeed, but not something anyone could be *expected* to obey.

At this seemingly discouraging moment, when the whole of Christ's teaching, not just his teaching on divorce, seems impossibly difficult, a stop and a fresh start can be made, for something significant has been said. Christ's claims can *not* be expected of us, except in those contexts of love where fairness is altogether transcended.[5] Divorce is not more nor less forbidden than hatred: it is something outside the Christian spirit. To be inside the Christian spirit, or rather to have the Spirit of Christ in ourselves, is no optional extra. It is what the Christian believes life is about, but it cannot be imposed upon us, even by the Church.

It has frequently been insisted that 'Christ did not legislate', but to put the matter so can be misleading, if it is then assumed that Christ's commands need not be obeyed. Christ was not accustomed to pronounce upon a man's rights: he propounded a better way in which God's will would be done and questions about rights could remain unasked. The rights remain, humanly speaking, as long as people are still concerned about them. What has been done in their name in the past does not have to be successfully undone as a condition for receiving God's grace now. Nor need Christians in Christ's name feel constrained to deny other people their reasonable rights. It is no more fair to require a man to forgive his adulterous wife than to require him to turn the other cheek or to give both coat and cloak. These things are not 'fair'; they are merciful, they are Christian, they are what God is asking us to become capable of. But we shall not make each other capable of them by abolishing lawsuits and divorce courts and impugning the legal validity of ordinary unregenerate human actions. There is no substitute for the fruit of the spirit. Christian ethics are a harvest: grown, not manufactured.

In all this I am still not making a distinction between Christian marriages and the unholy others. I am trying to distinguish between what can be demanded of someone and what he can do from love. The love which enables may not be recognizably the love of God. There are many loves which can draw people out of themselves: their friends, the causes they believe in, the things they make, their animals, their homes, and especially their own families. Humanly speaking, self-forgetfulness will always be partial and it is hopeless to pretend it is there when it is not, even when we think it ought to be there. Without it, we have to make do with fairness, until we can find the kind of inspiration which Christians believe is available for everyone in the love of God. To refuse such inspiration is not just a pity, it is death; but to presume upon it is legalism, bigotry and self-satisfaction. Some liberal views of marriage ask too little of grace; but some rigorist views are too prone to take it for granted.

Christians can get into a well-worn track here which may make them assimilate human love to divine love too quickly and risk losing both love and fairness. Besides believing that God's grace is available for married people and is somehow there even when things go wrong, they also believe that human love when all goes well is itself a small-scale image of God's love. They have biblical authority [6] for using marriage as a model for the grace of God, as parenthood is also an authorized model for the grace of God. So far, so good. The temptation is to try to build into the human side of these analogies something too large for them to hold, the infinite dependability which is part of the idea of God. When we are talking about God it seems easy enough to insist both that we can rely on His grace and also that we have no right to demand it. We are not expecting to put His right not to love us to any practical test. But when we are talking about human grace and it proves finite, the question has to be faced, Does it mean anything to say that grace must be free, that it is something we have no right to claim? If it does mean something, what are the consequences for those human relationships which are properly miniature forms of grace?

It is no wonder that when marriage or parenthood go wrong we are essentially confused about what to do, in a way in which we are not confused though we may be puzzled when straightforward rights conflict. There *is* something odd about claiming grace, divine or human, yet it is more needed than most things we can claim. We shall probably not get it by either permissive or legalistic short cuts. The problem of abortion is intractable for Christians in partly the same way as the problem of divorce, because the rights and wrongs of relationships of grace are founded upon paradox. It may be difficult to adjudicate in an ordinary quarrel, but we know what we are doing. When we allow a divorce or an abortion, we do not know what we are doing. Are we licensing adultery? Are we murdering a baby? Or are we only dissolving a contract that nobody wants, only using a drastic form of contraception? Few of us can be quite sure. Even when we take sides, the other picture is there to haunt us.

It may at least clarify our minds a little if we see the problems as essentially those of dealing in practice with a kind of absence of grace, over-simplified by both liberals and rigorists. Offspring are not parasites, marriages are not

64

business arrangements, so when they seem to have become so of course we are at a loss, and affirmation and counter-affirmation are no help. The nurture and care a new human being is going to need, like the 'mutual help, society and comfort that the one ought to have of the other' in marriage, go beyond what it is fair to demand, so we have abortions and divorces, but cannot get rid of the conviction that something sacred is being overthrown. To this sacredness a Christian ought to be particularly alert, and to the possible presence of God's grace in human situations; but his practical duty has still to be found and followed.

E

WHEN MARRIAGE FAILS

VII

JUSTICE

IF we can get rid of the notion that Christ abolished human marriage as a breakable contract and established Christian marriage as an unbreakable contract, and say rather that he reminded human beings of what marriage can be and is meant to be, we are in a position to see the real and formidable problems of the practical application of this teaching to our own times. It cannot be said that any of the Christian Churches has yet adequately answered the question of how to relate God's demands and God's mercy to the obstinate complexities of human lives. To many Anglicans (including the present writer) the Orthodox approach has a strong appeal [1]; but notoriously 'the grass is greener on the other side of the fence.' In all the Churches there are signs of a greater willingness to look at the problems afresh with both loyalty and flexibility, rather than to make a stand on entrenched positions.

Before entangling myself at last in these difficult matters, I should like to try to sort out something less recalcitrant. There is an area where the present approach to the theology of marriage, if it is adopted, can at once offer a greater clarity: the area of what *can* be humanly demanded, of marriage law and what the Church ought to think and say about it.

Some Christians suppose that a law of divorce is something which can only be contrary to the will of God, something which they must simply deplore and maybe campaign against. [2] When in practice such laws have to be made and administered they feel like apostates to be so conformed to the ways of the world that they acquiesce, as humane people, in these necessities. But they are by no means the first of God's people so to acquiesce. 'Moses for the hardness of your hearts suffered you to put away your wives.'[3] Even a theocratic state, if it has a developed institution of marriage, is liable to require a corresponding law of divorce. The bill of divorcement seen in context, like the law of 'eye for eye, tooth for tooth', is a requirement of order not a piece of permissiveness: its function is to set limits to human cruelty. A workable divorce law can be based on many possible fundamental principles, mutual consent, return of bride-price, unilateral repudiation, matrimonial offence, or 'breakdown of marriage'. When the safety valve of divorce is screwed up, arrangements for recognizing nullity are inclined to proliferate. The point is that to accept these facts, to recognize the divorce law of one's own country as humanly valid, to work for a juster divorce law even at the risk of making divorce easier not harder, is not disloyal to the teaching of Christ as we have it; for Christ did not repudiate but transcended Moses.[4]

What a divorce judge is doing is pronouncing upon rights, and any society has to make up its mind what these rights shall be. A wholly permissive society would have no need for a divorce law to set limits on rights. Free love means free separation; but the weak are likely to be better defended when some attempt is made to establish people's obligations and regulate their expectations of one another. It has not been found practicable by organized states to leave matters of sex and the family entirely to people's private arrangements. Yet the difficulty and paradox of trying to protect people against their natural protectors, their spouses or their parents, is such that a good family law[5] is particularly hard to achieve.

A Christian has no more, or less, right to say that the divorce law is not his business than to say that the law of tort is not his business. Individually he may be correct; but some Christians, in an imperfect world, have characteristically concerned themselves with justice for other people. The development of the English divorce law has not been an anti-clerical exercise. It has been a matter of attempts by churchmen and others to improve on existing arrangements for coping with hardness of heart. Divorce was not theoretically impossible nor non-existent before 1857. For better or worse, it was available by private Act of Parliament, which meant that it was available only to the rich and influential.[6] How this particular situation had arisen out of Reformation controversies about the meaning of the New Testament teaching is a complex matter of which a simplified account could only be tendentious.[7] What is significant for the present argument is that there were over three hundred of such divorces; that 'between 1830 and 1837 they were averaging over three a year'; and, still more remarkable, that 'the persons to whom the Acts referred appear not to have found difficulty in securing remarriage with the rites of the Church'.[8]

It is tempting for liberals to be triumphant at this and rigorists shocked and embarrassed, but they would be missing the point. Our forbears were not being careless of Christ's teaching: they were interpreting it in what seemed the obvious way. Divorce was forbidden 'saving for the cause of fornication'. It was this 'Matthaean exception' which governed the origins of English divorce law. The Parliamentary debates which led to the passage of the 1857 Act were conducted by churchmen thinking theologically. Their presuppositions were different from those of a church synod today, but they were just as religious. In the House of Commons Gladstone's explicit churchmanship was prominent but not out of place.[9] In the House of Lords the Bishops came into their own and debated the meaning of Christian teaching seriously and powerfully. The debates are conveniently summarized in Canon Winnet's account of them in *Divorce and Remarriage in Anglicanism* and it is an instructive exercise to trace the arguments which are still alive and those which have died. A curiosity to our way of thinking is the reluctance which was felt over allowing guilty parties to remarry at all. One might comment a little wryly, though without making an ethical judgment either way, that times have changed and it has lately been seen as a major social object in divorce law reform to allow more of them to do so. Mr. Abse in the House of Commons even attempted a theological appeal, speaking of numerous letters he received from people living in 'stable illicit unions' who asked (touchingly though with a somewhat naïve view of divine judgment), 'Before we meet our Creator, can we not ever regularize our union?' [10]

The upshot in 1857 of all the discussion was a law expressly based upon a literal understanding of one saying of Christ. That was how the 'matrimonial offence' became the basis of the English divorce law; and it needs to be said at once that this historical accident has not been a happy one. Humanly speaking it soon proved intolerable to allow divorce for adultery but for no other cause, and there has been constant and gradually successful pressure to enlarge the grounds, to include desertion, cruelty, and even, illogically enough, insanity. Theologically speaking Christians, working with the tools of Biblical criticism, have found with alarm or relief that the New Testament evidence cannot be interpreted in such a legalistic manner. However the 'Matthaean exception' is to be understood, it is no longer a curious little loophole in God's law. It might now seem the turn of rigorists to be triumphant and liberals abashed, and certainly since 1857 there has been a definite stiffening in the attitude of the Church on the indissolubility of marriage.[11] There has been an increasing tendency among many conscientious Christians to say 'Let the State do what it will. Our duty is to uphold our own law and teach our own members to live by it strictly.'

Yet there remains another more difficult but more constructive alternative to this turning away by the Church from what it has helped to make.[12] The 'Matthaean exception' has proved a broken reed. Perhaps what should go is not the whole idea of providing a proper law for hardness of heart, but the particular law which the Matthaean exception had suggested. It is tempting even to say that in 1857 a great opportunity was missed, an opportunity to think more theologically, not less, and to ground the divorce law not on unforgiven offences but on the impossibility of enforcing grace. Christ's claims go beyond what can be legally demanded, and hardness of heart still needs legislation. Bishop Thirlwall of St. David's understood this and suggested it in the House of Lords;[13] F. D. Maurice developed such an interpretation in a sermon in Lincoln's Inn;[14] Milton had once argued something like it;[15] but the Church did not listen effectively and became half committed to the notion that the least objectionable reason for divorce is that one spouse has sinned and the other is resolved to punish.

The present argument is rapidly leading, along the lines of the report *Putting Asunder* to which the present writer was a signatory, to the concept of breakdown of marriage as the most coherent basis for a law of divorce. It is however both just and a help in clarity to try to be fair to the idea of the matrimonial offence on the way. Lawyers like it because it is relatively easy to try, and this is far from being unimportant. It answers to rough-and-ready commonsense justice as a straightforward method of dealing with some of the most conspicuous cases of hardness of heart. Adultery, in particular, and in rather different ways desertion and cruelty, have been felt to cut at the root of marriage. We cannot demand that people shall put up with them: some redress must be available. It cannot just be called perverse that for centuries Christians took the 'Matthaean exception' as an authentic word of Christ, nor that they argued on the basis of St. Paul's words in I Corinthians[16] that desertion could also be an allowable ground for divorce. The human need for some recognition of these situations as long as life is being organized in terms of law is so great that it was easy to believe that the Lord himself expressly provided for such.

Nowadays it is easier to believe that the sort of thing the Lord himself taught was something more like the direct unqualified principle of Mark's gospel.[17] We may then go on to say that he left it to his followers to do the partly legal job of organizing a human society in which the harvest of the spirit can grow but cannot be forced.[18] The rules made by St. Paul, and probably the 'Matthaean exception' also, can be seen as examples of their setting about this task. We do not know what they did in practice. It is not clear whether St. Paul allowed divorce or only separation, nor what 'saving for the cause of fornication' (not adultery) meant in its context. The New Testament it seems gives Christians some early authority for thinking that such a legal task can be a proper one, but no blueprint for any particular divorce law.

So when the principle of the matrimonial offence turns out to work against common justice rather than for it there is no reason why Christians should not try to help their fellow countrymen to look for a better principle: 'better' in the sense of fairer and more consistent. This is what the *Putting Asunder* group was set up by the Archbishop of Canterbury to try to do. What is wrong with the 'matrimonial offence', as a century's experience showed, is its artificial insistence on one guilty and one innocent party. Perhaps there are cases where one spouse is entirely virtuous and the other wholly to blame, though it may be suggested that divorce with the right of remarriage is a curious remedy for such. But one might have expected Christians to have been among the first, not the last, to see that in the enormous majority of instances there is fault and excuse on both sides. What usually needs to be said is that something has gone wrong with the marriage, and that whatever actual offences have been committed on either side are symptoms rather than causes.

This interpretation was certainly indicated by the numerous anomalies which were constantly appearing in the English law in the years after the war. If the 'matrimonial offence' had answered to human realities better there would have been less frequent need for a 'discretion statement' in which the petitioner had to ask the court not to *refuse* a divorce because both sides had given cause for it. There would have been no need for the illogical but humane developments in the legal understanding of 'cruelty'[19] in which the respondent need have no animosity towards his spouse, he could even be insane, if his conduct gave rise to an intolerable situation. Insanity itself was always an awkward ground for divorce on the basis of matrimonial offence. Desertion on the contrary seemed a most clear-cut offence, but it is apt to be the most convenient cloak for divorce by consent; for why should a faithful deserted spouse who is simply wronged and does not condone the offence take proceedings for *divorce* at all? Even adultery need not always be the offence it seems; though the

74

notorious 'hotel cases', where out of lingering chivalry a man would adopt the role of 'guilty party' and let his wife divorce him, have been somewhat over-emphasized, to the indignation of responsible lawyers.

It was all these difficulties and anomalies taken together which revealed the inadequacy of a divorce law based upon offence. What brought the discontent to a head in the early sixties was a particular group of 'hard cases'. When the legally innocent spouse, who might be faithful and loving but who might be cold-hearted, shrewish or even revengeful, refused to institute divorce proceedings, the other could never be set free, even if the marriage has been humanly speaking an empty shell for years. Often the refusal was for deeply-felt reasons of conscience, but sometimes it was too easy to suspect that spite or at least self-righteousness was at work. Such imputations could only be damaging to the Church for the sake of whose teaching these refusals were being made.

At this stage the Church still seemed firmly committed to the law as it stood which made such rejection of divorce possible. What the Church was trying to uphold was the indissolubility of marriage. What it found itself upholding was the matrimonial offence. For many reasons good and bad, but certainly not simply obscurantist, it set itself strongly against the attempts which were being made[20] to deal with the hard cases in the most obvious way by adding an additional ground of long separation on to the existing grounds of offence and insanity.

Meanwhile the falsity of the position which insisted on the labelling of innocent and guilty was showing itself theologically, for the consciously innocent found it understandably hard to see why they at least should not be allowed to remarry in church. The state of the law, and the Church's 'so far and no further' attitude towards it, was no more satisfactory to rigorists than to liberals.[21] It made it much more difficult for people who wanted to uphold Christ's teaching strictly to explain that guilt or innocence had really nothing to do with it: remarriage was a sort of licensed bigamy which of course must not happen in church, however kind and charitable one tried to be in other ways to the people concerned.

Strange as it may be seem, the principle of breakdown as a basis for the law of divorce is more compatible with a whole range of theological ways in which Christians may understand 'indissolubility' than the principle of offence could ever be, and the Church of England seems to have been coming to see this. The report *Putting Asunder,* published in 1966 and welcomed by the Church Assembly in February 1967, recommended 'that the doctrine of the breakdown of marriage should be comprehensively substituted for the doctrine of the matrimonial offence as the basis of all divorce'.[22] This advice it offered to the State, both as conducive to justice and as acceptable to Christian thinking. The recommendation was not a capitulation to secular pressure. It was not an abandonment of the doctrine that marriage was indissoluble in favour of a new admission that it can break down. On the contrary, it was an attempt to arrive at a less superficial understanding of what divorce essentially is.[23]

Part of this understanding has to be a recognition 'that when a marriage comes to grief wounding cannot be avoided',[24] that a divorce law may be as fair as possible but cannot be ideal and is not likely to be painless. To base the law on breakdown requires the acceptance of three corollaries which are at the least difficult to explain and potentially unpalatable. Each of these corollaries was expressly allowed for in *Putting Asunder,* but each has been exaggerated in the way the law of England has in fact been changed, to an extent which must make a Christian hesitate in giving his approval.

The first of these corollaries is that the concept of a 'ground for divorce' cannot be wholly excluded. Marriages break down in specific ways, and often because spouses behave badly. The offences defined in the law as it was are at least highly relevant to any attempt to determine whether a marriage has broken down.[25] If breakdown has been established, the vexed question of maintenance cannot be decided without reference to guilt and innocence. 'Value judgments would still need to be made in this connection.'[26]

The *Putting Asunder* group had hoped though that no grounds need be expressly formulated in a new law, and that the court could try each case on its merits with a procedure analogous to an inquest on the marriage.[27] The kinds of decision which would have had to be made were not entirely without precedent in the existing law.[28] This suggestion proved too sanguine, and it does not seem necessary to think that the principle of 'breakdown of marriage' rather than of 'matrimonial offence' must absolutely stand or fall by it. It may be that 'inquest' was not an entirely satisfactory concept here in any case, as on the one hand an inquest presupposes a death, and on the other hand those hostile to Christianity, deprived of a chance to label the Church obscurantist, could instead assimilate 'inquest' to 'inquisition' and suggest that what was being proposed was a field-day for nosey parkers. In the event the Law Commission criticized *Putting Asunder* with promptitude and courtesy,[29] pointing out cogently that it was essential in practice to give divorce judges something more definite to go on; and a compromise was arrived at, in which the principle of breakdown was indeed comprehensively substituted for the principle of offence, but which required as evidence for breakdown that one or more of a list of specific situations should have arisen. This compromise became law on October 22nd, 1969.

Secondly, and more distressingly, if matrimonial offence is no longer to be the only basis for divorce, it has to follow that people may find themselves divorced when they have *not* committed offences, maybe when they are wholly innocent. This is part of what it means to say that marriages can break down.[30] It means that when any common life has permanently disappeared, there is no sense in pretending that the bond is still there. Such irretrievable breakdown is not to be presumed lightly. The law has fixed the criterion as five years' separation, and this seems realistic. What the law has not done is create the hurt. The breakdowns were happening and the

77

innocent were suffering already. They were suffering the desolation of the collapse of their marriages which they had wanted to maintain; and many women in this situation were suffering too from straitened and precarious financial circumstances which the State tried but often failed to ameliorate. The enforcement of proper maintenance for deserted wives even when there has been no divorce was always desperately difficult.

What the law has done is recognize that these breakdowns can happen and that in many cases the joint life is not going to be resumed. It has not prevented those who believe in a metaphysical bond over and above the joint life from continuing to act on this belief and reckoning themselves as still married; though it has withdrawn its encouragement from unrealistic clinging to the shadow when the human substance has long ago gone. To some faithfully religious people it should come as a relief not be under pressure to set free an erring spouse in the name of kindness.

The risk is that to recognize the hurt may after all, not create, but enlarge it, and especially that a law based on breakdown may seem to say to would-be erring spouses 'go and do likewise'. The *Putting Asunder* group in awareness of this risk made two stipulations for a just law based on breakdown. One was that people who were divorced through no fault of their own should have their financial rights protected.[31] It would be intolerable, for example, for a wife who has never chosen, wanted or deserved a divorce to lose not only her husband, whom the law cannot secure to her, but also her pension rights, which it can.

The second stipulation was that people who wanted divorces should not be allowed to take blatant advantage of their own wrong doing.[32] To prevent the law being abused in this way, it is necessary to say in some cases, not that a marriage has not broken down when patently it has, but that notwithstanding the fact of breakdown a divorce cannot be allowed because one spouse's conduct has been so outrageous that it would be against the public interest to countenance it. This bar has been partially built into the new English law:[33]

78

but the other stipulation has not fared so well. The court can indeed refuse a divorce if it is dissatisfied with the financial arrangements which have been made, and this is what is needed; but to the requirement of 'reasonable and fair' financial provision has been added the sinister qualification, 'or the best that can be made in the circumstances'.[34] This makes it legally possible to make essentially inadequate provision for a faithful first wife when there is not enough money available to support two families. Many of those who welcome the new law in principle must have serious qualms about whether the express acknowledgment of this possibility does not in itself constitute a grave injustice.

The third awkward corollary of the doctrine of breakdown sticks particularly in the throats of churchmen. The best evidence that a marriage has broken down must be that neither spouse wants to continue it. So it follows that the principle of breakdown of marriage has to include an element of divorce by consent. Some would draw the further conclusion that a law of divorce based on breakdown, by making marriage fundamentally terminable rather than permanent, is creating a kind of union no longer recognizable by Christians as valid marriage at all.

To this there are two answers, both indicated in *Putting Asunder*.[35] First, it must be pointed out that the old law also contained divorce by consent, but more inefficiently and less honestly. If husband and wife decided to have a divorce they could achieve it, but at the price of unedifying insincerities and complex manoeuvres. No law can or indeed should keep two people together who are determined to part. If this is 'divorce by consent', it is hardly the bogey it is made into.

Secondly, there is an essential but much overlooked distinction to be made here. Divorce by consent as the *basis* of the law must indeed be objectionable to Christian opinion, as making marriage into a dissoluble contract. The recognition of consent on the other hand in the sense of acquiescence as a crucial part of the *evidence* for breakdown leaves marriage in principle what it was under the law of matrimonial offence, a 'contract conferring status', intended to be permanent. The

79

distinction lies in whether a court has to try the issue of whether a marriage has broken down, or whether a divorce needs only to be registered if the spouses claim it in proper form. The Belgian law of divorce is based upon consent in this sense;[36] the English law is not, for it does not rest the permanence of marriage upon the mere will of the parties. Its two-year separation clause with acquiescence is no more true divorce by consent than its five-year separation clause is the unilateral repudiation allowed in classical Muslim law. Each is a way of proving breakdown, not of simply dissolving a contract. The court is not supposed just to take note of a set situation.[37] It may have further work to do and matters to determine, and it is meant to have regard for the stability of marriage, and the protection of the weak. Marriage remains in law as in Christian belief, 'the union of one man with one woman, voluntarily entered into for life'.

Regrettably, maybe disastrously, this distinction has been obscured by an amendment slipped into the Divorce Law Reform Bill in the House of Lords. The word 'consent' was substituted for 'does not object' as a stronger safeguard against abuse, and a door was opened for misunderstanding and deterioration. It can be alleged with relish or horror that divorce is now allowed in England on the ground of consent, and that marriage in English law has become essentially perishable. The trouble is that if this is believed widely enough it will at last become true. There are signs that instead of withstanding the confusion and carefully drawing the distinction between unacceptable and inevitable consent the Church is tending to succumb, to do its enemies' work for it, to accept and even widen a gulf which there need not have been between itself and the State. In the interests of everybody it would be better for it to keep its head, by all means to point out the unsatisfactory aspects of the new law, but to minimize them and still to hope they may be overcome. There is still a good opportunity to grasp the advantages both in theory and practice, in justice and in coherence, which a principle of breakdown has over an artificial and overgrown principle of offence.

VIII

MERCY

THE Divorce Reform Act 1969 came into operation on January 1st, 1971. Many churchmen have assumed that this must mean a widening gulf between Church and State not only in practice but in theory. They have jumped to the conclusion that the Church must reconsider its policy on marriage: either to reiterate its own law and explicitly repudiate the State's; or to amend its own teaching in response to contemporary thinking. Each of these reactions seems to indicate a failure of nerve.

On the one hand, to repudiate the law of the land at this juncture, when Christians have been allowed a considerable say in trying to make it humanly fair, and while it still plainly maintains lifelong marriage as the norm, could be a most retrograde step. What the State recognizes as marriage is the intention of monogamous union for life, and the fact that it is not unwilling to grant relief from this does not alter the meaning of the contract. Presumably the marriage at Cana which Christ adorned and beautified with his presence was legally capable of being dissolved by unilateral repudiation.

As Chancellor Garth Moore explained in a Memorandum submitted to the previous marriage commission, from which he has most kindly given me permission to quote: 'The ceremony and the words used at a Register Office have been and are as explicit on this point as the service in the Book of Common Prayer. . . . Both theologically and in law it is the intention of the parties at the time of the ceremony which makes the marriage, and in general, their intention can be judged only by their words.' He therefore gave his opinion that provided the words are not altered 'a valid marriage will continue to result despite the new Act'.

On the other hand, it is just as unwise to argue for a

81

relaxing of the Church's marriage discipline simply for the reason that divorce has been made easier by law. *Putting Asunder* emphasized strongly[1] that there is a distinction to be made here: 'How the doctrine of Christ concerning marriage should be interpreted and applied within the Christian Church is one question: what the Church ought to say and do about secular laws of marriage and divorce is another question altogether. This can hardly be repeated too often.' In accordance with this the Archbishop of Canterbury in his preface to the report affirmed his own conviction that if there were to be legislation along the lines suggested 'the Churches would still maintain their own pastoral discipline'. It would be both illogical and disloyal for one who signed the report to proceed forthwith to argue that the new situation, which *Putting Asunder* helped to bring about, in itself required a change in the Church's own teaching. In theory, even a strict rigorist could go along happily with *Putting Asunder* and still believe in *Christian* marriage as a metaphysical bond from which there could be no divorce.

If the Church sees fit eventually to reject rigorism and make a change in marriage discipline, that change must be due to theological thinking which was outside the terms of reference of *Putting Asunder*. As for the pastoral argument that it is up to the Church to do something for the unhappy people now to be divorced without their own consent, it is at least unsubtle to suggest that what should necessarily be done for them is remarriage in church. Indeed it might be argued that remarriage is particularly unsuitable here, for it makes more sense to say that these people are 'really' still married than anybody divorced under the old law.

Yet in spite of these arguments that the Church's position remains essentially the same, its marriage discipline is now in a thoroughly unstable condition. There is a great deal of discontent, much of it reasoned and realistic, with the existing policy, which is still to try to forbid remarriage in church while allowing those concerned back to Communion. Some people are no doubt consolidating their views but a great many are changing them, either hardening under contemporary pressures or softening the outlines of an earlier clarity in response to the complexity of the problem. The Commission which was set up in 1967 to 'prepare a statement of the Christian doctrine of marriage' consisted of variegated members some of them committed in print to differing views, but it formed a common mind and recommended that if the Church reached a moral consensus in favour of the remarriage of divorced people in church 'it would be compatible with reason, the word of God in scripture, and theological tradition.'[2] In this agreement the Commission has not proved to be a microcosm of the Church of England. The General Synod after several debates rejected its proposal that formal enquiry should be made in the dioceses whether such a consensus obtained;[3] and a new Commission has just been set up to reconsider the whole matter. It is said to have been 'given wide terms of reference to enable it to put forward a range of options'.[4] Unanimity seems hardly to be expected but eventually decision, positive or negative, is going to be required.

It would be pointless and impertinent for me simply to reiterate what the previous Commission said, but there still seems some value in attempting to explain and develop it a little in relation on the one hand to the positive view of marriage which I have been trying to put forward and on the other hand to the continuing controversy in the Church. If the new law in itself is no good reason for change, why is change so promptly being asked for? It looks as if the new law and the pressure within the Church are indeed related, not as reason and consequence but as *both* effects of fresh thinking on marriage. The question is whether this fresh thinking can be seen as a proper return to a less legalistic way of understanding Christ's teaching, or whether it is only a weak accommodation to short-sighted secular humanitarianism.

This chapter is called 'Mercy', but as the name of a problem not of an answer. To have mercy does not mean to yield. Mercy has to do with grace and understanding not with mere compliance. It is even harder to achieve than justice, and ought to mean more than either pity or compassion though it includes these and gives them prominence. In being called to bind and loose the Church is required to exercize God's mercy and may well feel this to be a terrifying task.

What is wrong with the present policy is not that it is illogical or lacking in compassion, but that it is not a policy. It is a way of evading the issue, of saying in the last resort neither Yes nor No.[5] It can deal really well with the easy cases, the people who have sinned in the past and are now repentant. For these it is both realistic and compassionate to say, as one would to the mother of an illegitimate child, that what matters now is to make the very best that can be made of the existing situation with the help of God's grace. Unless one is rigorist enough to believe that a second marriage is wholly void and its partners open and notorious evil livers it is the refusal of communion which would be hypocritical, not its availability.[6] But where the second wedding is not over and done with but still in prospect there is *no pastoral answer* unless the Church feels able to give a full prohibition. 'No' can be an answer and so can 'Yes'; 'I don't know' is sincere but if persisted in becomes idle; 'It is up to you to decide' sounds good but amounts in practice to 'Do this without God and then see if He will forgive you'. This is not an answer which the Church, which is supposed to speak for God, ought to have the face to make as a matter of policy.

In principle we are refusing to bless what Christ deplored; in practice we are refusing to make up our minds whether to affirm in Christ's name that certain actions must always be deplorable. To say 'Get through this crisis on your own and then come quietly back' looks like leaving people to their own devices at the moment of their greatest need. It may be lay people who can see this best because they are not being asked to remarry people but to encourage them. They are faced with the problem of whether it must always be the part of Christian loyalty to *dis*courage second marriages after divorce, to express regret, to refuse wedding invitations maybe and send no presents, even where humanly speaking there seems much cause to rejoice. It is not cowardice nor mere conformity that makes some of these cases seem quite different from straightforward 'living in sin' or infidelity to an existing marriage, where Christians may be reluctant to judge but know what the judgment ought to be.[7]

It is no wonder that one of the strongest of the present pressures is the pressure after all to separate Christian and non-Christian marriage. It is a tempting answer, because it promises to allow Christians to sympathize when people who do not owe allegiance to Christ divorce and remarry, acknowledging the validity of their proceedings but renouncing any such right for those who know the grace of God. It is argued that it would be much less confusing for everybody if the Church politely withdrew from secular marriage as it has now developed. Civil weddings for all are accordingly recommended, followed by church ceremonies only for those who want to be truly married in a Christian sense. So it is hoped some scandal and much distress could be avoided.

'The world does this: Christians do that': such a stance is straightforward but not subtle enough. In practice, it would essentially be an attempt to separate the tares and the wheat too soon. Among the recognizable extreme cases of faithful Christians entering consciously into indissoluble unions and explicit unbelievers wanting to keep their options open there is a tangled growth of mixed value including some tender shoots. If marriage in church were reserved for the faithful many people's latent faith would never come to fruition; others would presume on faith and find themselves trapped in legalistic bands; and where partners were uneven in their faith the Church of England would find itself newly saddled with the kind of problem of 'mixed marriages' with which the Roman Church is now afflicted.

In principle, the policy of separating Christian and non-Christian marriage is an over-simplification. It almost but not quite grasps the point that what marriage demands can be achieved only by grace (human grace though as well as divine) not by enforcement.[8] It completely misses the point that Christ's teaching on marriage is about the human institution which belongs to creation not specially to redemption.[9] It does not ask enough of the world at large, and of Christians

85

it will still seem to be asking too much because it is still asking it in a legalistic way.

But how can it be properly asked in any but a legalistic way? If Christ's comparison of re-marriage after divorce with adultery is to be taken seriously, it looks as if humanly speaking nothing can be done for those in insoluble marriage difficulties. The rejection of the idea of a special sort of marriage for Christians has meant that the problem cannot even be confined to dedicated believers who should have the resources to bear it.

At this stage one is bound to consider another answer which tries to do by nullity what it is deemed wrong to do by divorce. This approach may be no more than a policy of backing up a negative theory with a compassionate practice; but it has a good deal of interest because it has recently been enjoying a new lease of life. If Christ taught that re-marriage after divorce is literally impossible, it must appear that the only way in which one can show effective mercy to people in real trouble with their marriages is to find some way of saying that they have never been married at all; and there are numerous methods of setting about this. Some of these efforts have shown themselves both so legalistic and so open to abuse that they have become too easy a target for glib attacks. At their best they still deserve the responsible criticisms brought against them [10] that the nullity they allow is only juridically, not humanly and really, distinct from the divorce they condemn.[11]

What has been happening recently is that certain Roman Catholic scholars [12] who accept the premise that true marriage is utterly indissoluble have been considering more deeply the unreality of some unions which have proved only too dissoluble in fact. Of course many people, including many Christians, will not see the problem in this way because they will reject the total indissolubility of marriage, thinking of divorce as regrettable but still possible. But any serious ecumenical endeavour requires that the concept of indissolubility should be reckoned with. For such an endeavour the idea that some people are just not capable psychologically of forming a true

86

marriage seems full of promise when it becomes humanly apparent that the bond into which they have entered is incapable of being maintained. This idea can be expressed in terms of psychological nullity [13] or in a more complex way in terms of a sort of psychological non-consummation. Professor Bernhard argues,[14] for instance, that although the consummated marriage of Christians is indeed indissoluble, certain marriages never attain indissolubility in this sense and might be dissolved. This is a far cry from the legalistic hunting for impediments which has brought the 'nullity not divorce' answer into disrepute.

Yet if and in so far as it is still nullity not divorce which is indicated, this suggestion also is an over-simplification. It is hard to see how it can do what is asked of it in practice, for if people are to be deemed incapable of entering into a true marriage, this difficulty must beset the second union for the sake of which they are seeking to be free from the first. But worse, such an idea of nullity is likely to infect healthy marriages even more than the possibility of divorce. 'A man leaves his father and mother and cleaves to his wife, and they become one flesh.' Can human beings ever be sure that this is so? If indissolubility depends upon consummation and consummation is treated as a gradual achievement over many years, who may claim to have attained it? When divorce proves that such consummation was not attained, is one to say that there was no marriage or that there was a marriage which was not indissoluble? In the first case we must call no man married until he is dead, but in the second we have emptied the teaching of Christ of all content, for we have made divorce self-justifying: its occurrence goes to show that here is a case to which Christ's words about indissolubility do not apply.

It still seems best then to stress traditionally that it is consent not consummation which makes a marriage.[15] Two people take each other as man and wife. One can then appreciate all the facts which make it promising to say that true consummation of a marriage is a lifelong attainment, without being obliged, or allowed, to say if anything goes wrong that there

87

was never a marriage. This leaves divorce as something real which does not always collapse into nullity,[16] and therefore it gives point to Christ's saying 'What God has joined let not man put asunder'. It still needs to be insisted that this was not a platitude but a command.

So the problem remains, thornier than ever, what happens when the command is broken? How is God's mercy to be made practically available to those who are sinners in this particular way? The Church is apt to say, 'The teaching of Christ cannot be kept in the world but it can be kept in the Church'. What it should say is, 'It cannot be kept except as fruit of the spirit'.[17] There are times when even Christians may have to make do with fairness, for the fruit of the spirit cannot be simulated and must not be presumed upon, *even in the Church*. What is the Church to do on behalf of Christ when it has already failed, for some people, to provide a context in which these transcendent commands can be truly kept? For the Church to try to separate itself from the sin of divorce has indeed the moral attractiveness of Pharisaism but may come under the same condemnation.

This means that the pressure to offer some positive blessing to people attempting remarriage after divorce is not entirely an accommodation to 'progress' but is rather an appeal to the Church to take some responsibility for what it is not willing absolutely to forbid. This is the way which has long been followed in the Orthodox Churches; and one of the main conclusions of the report *Marriage, Divorce and the Church* was that the East has a great deal to teach the West here.[18] The western tradition has seemed to insist that whereas Christ was wont to repudiate dichotomies his followers must be legalistic *or* permissive. This is still the tradition in which Anglicans have been formed and from which they cannot readily escape; it looks as if in practice they must decide to be rigorists or liberals; but maybe they can, as it were, look between the bars in the direction in which freedom would lie, towards a situation in which the Church would have such a strong positive doctrine of what marriage can be that it could afford to be compassionate to the failures.

Canon Allchin has argued this in an inspiring appendix which he contributed to *Marriage, Divorce and the Church,* in which he asked what accounts for the difference between East and West at this point.[19] 'I believe', he said, 'it is a deep but not easily expressed difference about the nature of the activity of God. . . . Eastern theology has always insisted on maintaining the freedom and transcendence of God who goes beyond all our concepts and can never be limited by them.' He is 'a God of order and of faithfulness. But he is also a God of many plans, of infinite possibilities, who is not defeated by man's sin, nor bound even by laws which expressed his will. His wisdom is many sided, and we do not comprehend it. . . . It is this God that the Church serves, His love and forgiveness which it is to make present in the world.'[20] This way of thinking is no newfangled and tendentious attempt to squeeze Christ's teaching into the twentieth century, but the response of a great Christian tradition to the perennial sinfulness of man in the light of God's mercy.

But if the Church can offer people God's blessing when they try to reshape their lives after marital catastrophe, it must consider with all carefulness what form this blessing may take. The commission which produced *Marriage, Divorce and the Church* was not able to draw any distinction of principle between a 'service of blessing' and the use of the full marriage service. Either is a matter of the Church countenancing a union in God's name. Yet many people who feel that some sort of blessing could be offered are still horrified at the idea of using the marriage service itself a second time for people who have broken their first vows. It is worth trying to disentangle the issues here a little, making the assumption for which I have been arguing so far that *some* blessing can be appropriate, that to approve a second union as the best outcome in the circumstances is not necessarily to make oneself an 'accessory to sin'.[21]

The strongest objection is generally to the re-use of the vows. Is it not a blasphemous mockery to promise a second time to a different person 'to love and to cherish, till death us do part, according to God's holy ordinance'? If many people feel this then there is no 'consensus' in the Church for allowing it to be done, whichever way the theological argument goes. Yet feelings, even righteous feelings, can get out of hand, and horror at the breaking of past vows is a strong feeling which could confuse the issue. If one believes that a promise is not exactly a statement but an action,[22] one must take seriously the fact that promises create marriages and that to attempt to create a new marriage is essentially to make promises, implicitly or explicitly, however frail they may now be deemed to be. To make the new promises explicitly is honesty, not hypocrisy. It does not break the old ones afresh but brings home the seriousness of the new. It is for the second spouse to consider whether trust is possible, not for the congregation who are present as witnesses not as judges.

There are two still more serious objections to the straightforward re-use of the Church's marriage service: that it would erode the meaning of the service when it is used for the *first* time and make all marriage vows conditional,[23] and that it would hopelessly obscure Christ's teaching that marriage is meant to be lifelong.[24] In essence both these objections will have to be accepted, although a little can be said to mitigate them. There is no need to go so far as to say that the known possibility of divorce makes marriage vows 'conditional'; the lawyer's word 'defeasible' could be more accurate.[25] Vows which were truly meant to be permanent can be *defeated*, or *frustrated* to use another legal analogy, admittedly approximate, suggested in *Marriage, Divorce and the Church*.[26] Of course divorce weakens marriage but as long as permanence remains the norm marriage vows do not lose their meaning.

But still for the Church officially to allow the use of the full marriage service after divorce without demur would, in practice and maybe in theory, go a long way towards destroying the norm. To give the impression that the Church no longer cares about Christ's teaching would be more cruel in the long run to those who have never been divorced than the present policy ever is to those who have. The Eastern Orthodox churches supply an alternative penitential form of service for all second marriages; but it seems that this is not always used.[27] In any case, what matters here is not that penitence should be apparent but that mercy should. In blessing divorced people in the making of new unions it is imperative that the Church should make it clear that this is a special dispensation not an ordinary means of grace. That is why the authors of *Marriage, Divorce and the Church* proposed, not services of blessing without vows, not wedding services with a penitential cast throughout, not the Prayer Book solemnization of matrimony without comment, but instead of all these the full service prefaced with a declaration by the priest of just what is being done.

Of this recommendation and of the way in which it is formulated many criticisms have been made, some better founded than others. The role of the preliminary announcement has been widely misunderstood and its penitential character exaggerated, as if a sort of wallowing in remorse had been suggested instead of a humble but businesslike acknowledgment of imperfection. The extension of the legal principle of 'frustration' has also been taken too literally. Its function was not to produce a quasi-juridical excuse for the breaking of marriage bonds, but to suggest that where the human bond had already been broken there might be literally nothing left towards which fidelity in any literal sense could be properly directed.[28] It has also been objected that too great a burden would be laid upon the clergy; but Anglican clergy ought to be as well able to undertake this pastoral task as Free Church ministers are at present. They are already having to consider questions about re-admission to Holy Communion. It would not be a matter of deciding guilt or innocence in the past or of making forecasts for the future, but rather of making sure that people understood what they were asking for and what was being offered them in God's name. Even sincerity is something which can grow.

Of many critics of the proposal, two particularly stand out: Mr. John Lucas writing in *Theology*,[29] who put the rigorist case at its most cogent; and Dr. Graham Leonard, Bishop of Truro, in the Mothers' Union report *New Dimensions*, who raised important questions which will be best looked at in the next chapter. Mr. Lucas' courteous and trenchant review of *Marriage, Divorce and the Church* deserves a full reply in the like spirit.

It was a pity that he felt it necessary to begin[30] by brushing aside the 'glosses and qualifications' with which the Commission attempted to safeguard its controversial recommendation; for these 'glosses and qualifications' were not included as a sop to critics but as constituting the differentia of what we felt bound to say. Evidently we were walking a knife edge between rigorism and permissiveness. We came to see the best path as running along the liberal side of the ridge. From those who think we have gone too near the edge we need a steadying hand not a push over. Of course this route is precarious but the more the dangers of permissiveness are seen the more needful it is to emphasize not belittle the qualifications we tried to insist upon.

It may be that after all the fact will have to be faced that here as elsewhere qualifications are useless and the Church must choose between extremes. It will be a shame if among Christians this must be so, for the rigorist view is as ugly without its qualifications as the liberal view is woolly. The 'what will come over' argument cuts both ways: for everyone who is encouraged by liberal Christians to suppose that marriage is no longer for life, there must be someone who is led by rigorism to think that matrimonial errors are the sin against the Holy Ghost. The rigorist finds it as hard to show that he hates only the sin and loves the sinner as the liberal finds it to show that he really believes in the permanence of marriage.

Mr. Lucas argued that 'the choice is stark'; that 'the perceptions of the public are crude and unsubtle: and therefore social institutions have to be simple and unambiguous'.[31] The Lord seems not to have thought so when he healed on the Sabbath, nor when he laid himself open to misunderstanding by eating with publicans and sinners. St. Paul had to involve himself in niceties of argument about circumcision and meats offered to idols. Where the facts are complex one is not going to be allowed the luxury of simplicity nor of being readily comprehended.

But suppose after all that the facts are simple? Many critics will still undoubtedly feel that since Christ plainly forbade divorce, any attempt to get round this awkward fact is just special pleading. We must have rigorism if we are to call ourselves Christians at all. 'Christ never taught us that we should give in to ourselves, nor called us to a soft life.' [32] This was the real substance of Mr. Lucas' attack on the Report, and certainly he has a strong case, just as the out-and-out pacifist has a strong case. He complained[33] that 'Our Lord's teaching is dealt with in an appendix'[34] and that the arguments in the body of the Report are an easy capitulation to the persuasiveness of the hard cases without ever facing the strength of the rigorist position. His criticism is telling; but I think that he has not after all succeeded in being fair. The position the Commission tried to put is more subtle. It can be stated something like this: The Lord had a very high doctrine of marriage and taught that in its nature it is permanent, but to say that in all circumstances he 'forbade divorce' is to go beyond the evidence. The doubt about exactly what he meant Christians to do in hard cases goes right back into the New Testament itself, with the 'Matthaean exception' and the 'Pauline privilege'.[35] The duty to take his teaching extremely seriously does not involve the belief that rigorism as such is proved by the New Testament, and to find out what it does involve wider arguments must be used, which are used in the body of the Report. The specific discussion of the biblical evidence was not so to speak relegated to an appendix but rather entrusted to one, for the whole Commission did not share the necessary specialized knowledge.[36]

In these difficult matters of course we must consider the 'whole thrust of the New Testament',[37] but this is exactly what the Report sought to do. It is fair to say that one of the most conspicuous features of the teaching of Christ was a refusal to be put in pigeon-holes, and that his most characteristic moral move was the breakthrough.[38] It seems to have been wholly in keeping with all we know of him that when

asked about divorce he immediately talked about marriage;
it is regrettably equally in keeping with much of the history
of the Church that a commission whose terms of reference
were to prepare a statement of the Christian doctrine of
marriage should have found it necessary to talk so much
about divorce.

Of course the risk one runs when one tries to be subtle
is that one may fall into a sophisticated speciousness. Rather
than this Mr. Lucas prefers clarity. He believes that 'the
Western rather than the Eastern position is the true one',[39]
though it has 'no answer'[40] to the pastoral questions of what
people are really meant to do. He insists that the relationship
of marriage has 'the same indelible character that blood-
relationships have';[41] and here in one argument he shows
both the strength and the weakness of his stand, its integrity
and its need to omit complexities. He uses adoption as an
illustration to show by contrast how he understands the
marriage bond, but seems unwary of the extent to which it
complicates his position. 'The adoptive relationship', he says,
'may blossom and be blessed with every happiness . . . but
still the natural one remains, and may acquire suddenly great
significance'.[42] Mr. Lucas insists then that 'a marriage, like a
blood-relationship . . . can never be completely expunged';
but the argument must turn in his hand, unless he is prepared
to forbid adoption for fear of impugning blood relationships.
Like an adoption, a second marriage after divorce is evidently
something. It is not fair to say that people 'mouth the marriage vows a second time in church' any more than they
mouth the words 'my son' or 'my daughter' about an adopted
child. The Church must continue to insist that second marriage
after divorce is based on sin and requires penitence in a way
in which adoption is in no way based on sin; but the usefulness of the analogy is that in each case a new reality can, we
see in practice, be built on something a purist will have to call
pretence.

Sooner or later the Church will have to choose; but it will
choose liberalism at its peril if it forgets what rigorism at its
best is about, 'the radical change of outlook (*metanoia*) that

94

Christ spoke of',[43] which is honest in asking for forgiveness because it does not pretend that sin is not sin. The pressing practical question is by what kind of witness this change of heart can best be fostered. I have been trying to argue that it is by building up the norm but being frank about the continuing human need for exceptions that the Church can truly witness to Christ's teaching on marriage.

IX

DANGERS AND HOPES

THE most redoubtable opponent of the proposal to remarry divorced people in church has been the Bishop of Truro, Dr. Graham Leonard. In his diocesan synod and in the General Synod,[1] in the correspondence column of *The Times*[2] and most systematically in an appendix to the Mothers' Union report *New Dimensions*, he has criticized *Marriage, Divorce and the Church* from a rigorist point of view. He seems to have taken the very unanimity of its authors as a point against them,[3] discounting their statement of how agreement was gradually reached[4] and looking on them as a pressure group arriving at foregone conclusions. Yet if one can still appreciate the strength of the conviction that remarriage in church would be both wrong and dangerous, one can see that rigorists have a right to be concerned that their case shall not go by default because one commission has reached a common mind.

Rigorists still feel strongly and understandably that the view of marriage expressed in *Marriage, Divorce and the Church* substitutes the flimsy tie of 'relationship' for the solid bond of union and so subjects the permanence of marriage to people's passing whims. 'I take thee to my wedded wife to have and to hold from this day forward until the death of the relationship.' Against any such tendency Dr. Leonard insists that marriage is a *state*.[5] 'The permanence of this union is not something which is to be created as the marriage develops, but is of the very nature of the married state into which the couple enters by the exchange of mutual lifelong vows.' 'Some of us', he adds, 'have had traumatic evidence in our pastoral work of what happens when the existence of the marriage bond is made to rest upon the quality of the relationship. In the first place, who is to judge whether the relationships are sufficiently mature and deep to warrant the belief that the marriage still "exists"?'

Accordingly the more rigorist members of the Mothers' Union Commission of which Dr. Leonard was Chairman firmly rejected 'the idea that, when marriage relationship has broken down irretrievably, the marriage as such has ceased to exist'.[6] They pointed out that if a child 'is educated for marriage *solely* in terms of personal relationships, ignoring the structure, bond or *vinculum* of his marriage . . . he will . . . fail to develop as a married person himself and to equip his children for their task of family-making in the future'.[7]

Important as this point is, it contains an element of mis-understanding. It assumes that a relational view of marriage must run together two opinions which in fact a little more care could separate. The first of these is the view that what matters most in marriage is relationship, not for instance physical attraction for its own sake nor procreation for its own sake. The second is the view that the bond of marriage can in the last resort be sundered. When these are confused it is fatally easy to arrive at the position that marriages live or die with the quality of their relationships and that a little withering of the plant is proof that it is really dead. This view may be dangerously gaining ground and rigorists may be right to fear it; but it is not the same as the view that marriage is *for* relationship and that therefore if the relationship has wholly gone there is no moral point in continuing to maintain the bond. The bond does not wither of its own accord: it has to be cut. Marriage is indeed a state and a state which can outlast many vicissitudes, but not a 'meta-physical' state which persists whatever human beings do. Divorce is like induced abortion, not miscarriage; it is like switching off a machine when it is judged that conscious life can never return.

But to say all this by no means disposes of the whole of Dr. Leonard's case. He impressively insists upon the possi-bility 'that the one way in which the Church is today called to fulfil its duty to all men, is by training and enabling its members who are the Church to witness fearlessly to Christian

97

G

faith in their lives',[8] not by giving way to their unregenerate wants. A partial answer to such a rigorist stance over divorce is the earlier argument of this book, that grace cannot be enforced even in the Church; but it is not a complete answer because Dr. Leonard also differs strongly and explicitly from this very way of understanding grace. *Marriage, Divorce and the Church*, he says,[9] 'seems to adopt a view of grace far removed from that of the New Testament, which presents it as firmly linked to life in the Body of Christ, and to acceptance of the Lordship of Christ. In other words, the Commission seems to substitute an idea of the sustaining providence of God for the New Testament belief that grace and truth come through Jesus Christ.'

This is a serious criticism. It amounts to the charge that any recognition of the possibility of divorce among Christians is defeatist and fainthearted and so unfaithful to the Lord. Is Christianity after all supposed to make no real difference? Is the Christian community not the place where people *can* transcend the old morality of rights and claims? Is 'in Christ' a meaningless expression? Does our morality not take its rise from a live relationship with him? And if so, what is all this talk of not managing to obey His teaching?

It has to be admitted that liberalism is prone to tell us comfortably what we can do 'in the spirit of Christ' while in effect evading the issue of whether and where that spirit is to be found. For example, it is a temptation if one wants to reject rigorism to seize and as it were short-circuit Professor Jeremias' profound account of the meaning of the Sermon on the Mount in which he insisted that *'The Gospel preceded the demand'*.[10] It is easy to receive this joyfully by saying, 'Yes indeed. Without the Gospel the demand makes no sense', and never face the main point: 'the old aeon is passing away. . . . And now you should know: this is what life is like, when you belong to the new aeon of God. This is what sonship is like. This is what a lived faith is like.' [11] If we simply do not know, then we are not Christians at all.

First it may be said that we do know, a little; and that there is and has been through nineteen centuries such a thing as living in the Christian spirit. Christ's teaching on marriage is faithfully and happily kept in many marriages, both by those who can explain its meaning and by those who cannot. The more true this is, the less it can be used in argument, for modesty and unselfconsciousness will prevail. It begs the question to proclaim a victory unless there is a visible struggle. What Austin Farrer called 'the union of duty with delight'[12] cannot be made matter for boasting.

What remain for liberal and rigorist to argue about are the cases where duty remains duty and seems impossibly hard to keep. At this point the liberal surrenders and lets the new life go by default, while the rigorist seems equally to miss the point by saying, 'Lead the new life—*or else* . . . '. Suppose instead that Professor Jeremias' principle can be taken seriously without being short-circuited. *'Something pre-ceded.'*[13] Then we may say that the liberal is right that we cannot enforce the demands before the Gospel, and that the rigorist is right that in the end the demand cannot be evaded. So what we are asking for is a much more patient and humble rigorism, which will acknowledge the evident human in-adequacy of the Church and understand that even for some officially Christian people the Gospel is not yet real. So the problem is not to lay rules of perfection upon them but to build up the Christian community so that the harvest of the spirit can grow. The longest way round is the shortest way home, but a very long way round it may seem. Divorce and remarriage remain meanwhile as a sort of interim ethic, a witness to the imperfections of the Church, a warning against self-righteousness. While they last the Church takes some responsibility for them, and ought to do this explicitly. Where it really looks as if in a particular situation remarriage is humanly best, Christians need not shut their eyes to this fact in Christ's name. The penitential context of such remarriages must remain, but it is a corporate at least as much as an individual penitence which is in question.

Building up the Christian community so that people may become more capable of faithfulness to God and one another is not a simple planning exercise, nor one which can be done

99

by a bulldozer. 'Fellowship' cannot be laid on and the attempt to do so may debase it,[14] but it can be wisely created. The most promising way to try to build up Christian love is not to talk about commuity, however sincerely, but to get into the habit of thinking of other people as God's children, and to encourage them to think of themselves as such. 'Encouragement' could be a key word here, not in any soft or sentimental sense, but as literally imparting courage to people to be their own best selves, whether by spiritual sustenance, material help, or unadorned human goodwill. Christians ought to be able to offer this encouragement to one another and to the world in God's name; and they would be much more likely to elicit real repentance, turning again, than by offering a sort of schedule of demands. So Christian faith could be nurtured, and Christian people would indeed have something definite to which they could 'witness fearlessly' in their lives.[15]

But still to say 'some*thing* definite' could miss part of the point. Christian fidelity is faithfulness to a person not to an idea.[16] That is what has gone wrong with some Christian attempts to uphold the sanctity of marriage: there is something fundamentally Pharisaical, though in the best sense, about such loyalty. It witnesses, maybe nobly, to a principle, but there seems to be no love in it, neither the love of husband and wife for better or worse, nor the love of Christ who gives what he commands.[17] Without the love the witness is meaningless and counter-productive. The Church would do better not to require the witness, but to go back yet again to its task of finding and trying to comprehend the love.

This indicates the answer to Dr. Leonard's most telling point, that liberals too easily 'urge "the Church" to forgive' and miss 'the personal obligation to forgive which is laid upon every Christian'. He appeals eloquently and convincly for 'a far deeper and more searching examination of the meaning of forgiveness', and asks whether it can ever be said 'that for the *Christian* the marriage vows can no longer be fulfilled?'[18] Here he seems to allow too little, as *Marriage, Divorce and the Church* maybe allowed too much, to the idea of frustration. It *can* sometimes be said that the marriage vows can no longer be fulfilled, when there is no longer any question of fidelity to the *person* to whom they were made as distinct from the fact of having made them. It is right for the Church to say 'Be faithful in your marriage even if you have to forgive unto seventy times seven'. It is right for the Church to uphold people who say 'I will live without marriage for the love of God' whether their reason is positive vocation or previous failure. It is something quite different and more questionable to say 'You must live a single life although you have no vocation to celibacy because you are tied in a bond you cannot see nor do anything positive to cherish'. When that is the situation, it is honesty as much as compassion which suggests the alternative advice, 'Start where you are and do the best you can. A fresh beginning is not something easy, but you have the advantage of knowing how much you need God's grace. Make your new promises wholeheartedly, and be thankful.'

Whatever the Church decides it ought to say, it is likely to be misunderstood. If it is rigorist, it will be thought unforgiving. If it is liberal, it will be thought to abandon Christ's teaching. If it tries to explain a more subtle view, it will be thought to be liberal or rigorist. If it sets up practical safeguards there will be pressure to remove them. All that can be said is that the risks are great on all sides, so the only thing to do is what ought to be done anyway, consider what is right and then consider how best to explain it. Certainly if the Church does not come to some definite decision it will have the worst of both worlds. Its present policy loyally put into effect is not escaping, and I believe cannot escape, the taint of legalism; and unless it can be established afresh it will not continue to be loyally put into effect. There will be more dissentients who feel obliged to go ahead with remarriage in church without tarrying for any, without the corporate backing which alone can make such remarriage theologically justifiable. Human pity is a poor substitute for the mercy of God offered by the Church speaking in His

101

name. Meanwhile the world will lose interest in mercy and pity and will go its own way, looking for secular blessings and claiming rights. So in the end it could lose by default one of the greatest of all the secular blessings in God's creation, the human institution of faithful monogamous marriage in which total trust is built up over a span of years into a bond experienced as unbreakable.

NOTES

I. TOTAL COMMITMENT

1 Mark 10:6-8.
2 See below pp. 47-8.
3 *Essays in Orthodoxy*, pp. 281-4. Cf. *Marriage, Divorce and the Church*, Appendix 4, p. 128.

II. HUMAN INSTITUTION

1 See above, p. 18.
2 See *Marriage, Divorce and the Church*, Appendix 5, pp. 139-40. See below, p. 47. Cf. Paul Ramsey, *Deeds and Rules in Christian Ethics* (American edition), p. 45.
3 *The Council and Reunion*, p. 84 (italics mine).
4 *Ibid.*, p. 145.
5 See below, pp. 55-6.
6 *Marriage, Divorce and the Church*, paragraph 34. Cf. G. R. Dunstan, 'The Marriage Covenant', reprinted in *Theology*, May 1975, p. 251.
7 I have tried to work this out in *Incarnation and Immanence*.
8 Cf. *Marriage, Divorce and the Church*, paragraph 35 and Appendix 4, pp. 127-8.
9 e.g. 'Sketch for a personalistic universe' in *Human Energy*, p. 63.
10 See below, Chapter III. Cf. *Marriage, Divorce and the Church*, paragraphs 31 and 66, and Appendix 4, pp. 126ff.
11 See below, pp. 79-80.
12 See Austin Farrer. Wedding sermon in *A Celebration of Faith*.

III. WORKING MODEL

1 Above, p. 25.
2 e.g. Mark 8:35, John 12:24, I Corinthians 15:36.
3 See below, p. 33f.
4 See Ian Crombie in *Faith and Logic* (ed. Basil Mitchell), p. 75.
5 In *Incarnation and Immanence*.
6 In a review of a book on F. D. Maurice in *Theology*, October 1965.
7 Cf. Helen Oppenheimer, *The Character of Christian Morality*, p. 51.

8 Cf. Helen Oppenheimer, 'Moral Choice and Divine Authority' in *Christian Ethics and Contemporary Philosophy*, ed. I. T. Ramsey, p. 233.
9 Cf. *Incarnation and Immanence*, p. 173. *Marriage, Divorce and the Church*, Appendix 4, pp. 127-8, 129.
10 Cf. *ibid.*, Appendix 4, p. 129.
11 Cf. *ibid.*, paragraph 31 and Appendix 4, p. 128.
12 Cf. *Incarnation and Immanence*, p. 174.
13 I have argued this more at length in two other places: simply, in a pamphlet called *Christian Marriage* published in the SPCK 'Christian Knowledge Booklets' (1965), pp. 5ff.; and more technically in *Incarnation and Immanence*, Chapter 2.
14 Cf. *The Character of Christian Morality*, p. 80.
15 This way of thinking is of course profoundly indebted to Dr. Sherwin Bailey.
16 See *Marriage, Divorce and the Church*, Appendix 4, p. 129f., where I have said a little more about a 'theology of parenthood'.
17 Ephesians 5:21-33.
18 In an editorial in *Theology*, April 1975.
19 Dr. Sherwin Bailey sometimes seems on the brink of implying this, e.g. *The Man-Woman Relation in Christian Thought*, pp. 275-6.
20 See *Incarnation and Immanence*, pp. 192ff.

IV. SOCIAL REALITY

1 In the sense illuminatingly discussed by Dorothy Emmet in *Rules, Roles and Relations*.
2 Cf. 'Ought and Is' in *Duty and Discernment*, ed. G. R. Dunstan.
3 Cf. *Marriage, Divorce and the Church*, Appendix 5, pp. 139-40. See above, p. 23.
4 Cf. Austin Farrer. Wedding sermon in *A Celebration of Faith*.
5 See above, pp. 40ff.

V. INDISSOLUBLE BOND

1 See below, Chapter VIII.
2 *Theology*, May 1975.
3 *Ibid.*, p. 228.
4 See e.g. *Marriage, Divorce and the Church*, Appendix 1.
5 Mark 10:11 (A.V.).
6 Ephesians 5:32.
7 *The Man-Woman Relation in Christian Thought*, p. 115.
8 See A. R. Winnet, *The Church and Divorce*, p. 10.
9 Ronald Atkinson, *Sexual Morality*, p. 69, quoted because it is such an excellent introduction for moralists to philosophical ways of thinking as such.

[10] E. Schillebeeckx, *Marriage: Secular Reality and Saving Mystery*, I, p. 226.

[11] One fruit of this 'new look' has been the Agreed Statement on Eucharistic Doctrine produced by the Anglican-Roman Catholic International Commission; but this has behind it a great deal of more detailed exposition and discussion by both Catholic and Protestant scholars. To give adequate references would be to compile a bibliography of eucharistic theology. Here, I hope, it will be enough to specify one article which crystallizes this line of thought: Austin Farrer 'The Eucharist in I Corinthians' in *Eucharistic Theology Then and Now*.

[12] *Theology*, May 1975 (in a symposium with John Lucas and the present writer).

[13] *Ibid.*, pp. 230ff.

[14] Schillebeeckx, I, pp. 203-4; II, pp. 68-70.

[15] *Ibid.*, II, p. 68.

[16] Cf. Sherwin Bailey, *Common Sense about Sexual Ethics*, p. 60, who urges that Augustine's view has not received the attention it deserves.

[17] Macquarrie, *Theology*, May 1975, p. 236.

[18] Cf. J. Bowker, *Marriage, Divorce and the Church*, Appendix 2, p. 105.

[19] See H. Hart, 'On the ascription of responsibility and rights' in *Logic and Language*, I (ed. A. Flew), pp. 148ff.

[20] I have put this at more length in *Law and Love*.

[21] *The Marriage Covenant*, reprinted in the same number of *Theology*, May 1975 (pp. 249-50).

[22] See above, p. 49.

VI. HARVEST OF THE SPIRIT

[1] Mark 10:11 (A.V.).

[2] See above, p. 18.

[3] Cf. *Law and Love*, p. 71f. See the little *Report of the Joint Committees* of the Convocations of Canterbury and York in consultation with members of the marriage Commission in 1971. In the last section of this a number of anonymous but typical 'difficult cases' are set out without comment but with some of the pastoral and theological questions they raise.

[4] Matthew 23:4. (A.V.).

[5] Cf. *The Character of Christian Morality*, Chapter VIII.

[6] Ephesians 5:31-2.

VII. JUSTICE

[1] See below, pp. 88-9.

[2] Cf. *Putting Asunder*, paragraph 11 (foot).

[3] Cf. *ibid.*, paragraphs 12-13.

[4] Cf. *ibid.*, paragraph 16.
[5] Cf. the Law Commission report *Reform of the Grounds of Divorce, The Field of Choice*, paragraph 15.
[6] See *Putting Asunder*, Appendix A, paragraph 13.
[7] *Ibid.*, Appendix A, paragraph 7ff.
[8] *Ibid.*, Appendix A, paragraph 8.
[9] A. R. Winnet, *Divorce and Remarriage in Anglicanism*, p. 143.
[10] *Hansard*, House of Commons, February 9th, 1968.
[11] *Putting Asunder*, Appendix A, paragraph 15.
[12] Cf. *ibid.*, paragraphs 11, 20, 21.
[13] A. R. Winnet, *Divorce and Remarriage in Anglicanism*, pp. 139-40 and note. *Putting Asunder*, Appendix A, paragraph 11.
[14] *Putting Asunder*, paragraph 16.
[15] In his pamphlets on divorce 1643-5.
[16] I Corinthians 7:15.
[17] Mark 10:9.
[18] Cf. G. R. Dunstan. Editorial in *Theology*, May 1975 and *The Artifice of Ethics*, p. 29.
[19] *Putting Asunder*, paragraph 50 and note.
[20] In 1951 by Mrs. Eirene White and in 1963 by Mr. Leo Abse.
[21] Cf. *Putting Asunder*, paragraph 43.
[22] *Ibid.*, paragraph 26.
[23] e.g. *ibid.*, paragraphs 40-1, 45, 54-5 and Appendix D.
[24] *Ibid.*, paragraph 65 (p. 49).
[25] Cf. *ibid.*, paragraph 80.
[26] *Ibid.*, paragraph 91.
[27] e.g. *ibid.*, paragraphs 28, 62.
[28] e.g. *ibid.*, paragraph 49.
[29] *Reform of the Grounds for Divorce: The Field of Choice* published in November 1966.
[30] e.g. *Putting Asunder*, paragraph 65.
[31] *Ibid.*, paragraphs 29, 64.
[32] *Ibid.*, paragraphs 29, 66.
[33] Divorce Law Reform Act 1969 4(1) and (2)b.
[34] *Ibid.*, 6(2)b.
[35] *Putting Asunder*, paragraphs 32, 47-8, 59, 60. Cf. *Incarnation and Immanence*, p. 173.
[36] *Putting Asunder*, Appendix B, paragraphs 2-6.
[37] Divorce Law Reform Act 2(2) (3), 3(1) (2), 4.

VIII. MERCY

[1] Paragraph 6.
[2] *Marriage, Divorce and the Church*, p. xii.
[3] November 1974.
[4] *The Times*, October 14th, 1975.
[5] See above, p. 13.
[6] Cf. Helen Oppenheimer, *Law and Love*, p. 76.
[7] See above, pp. 61-2.
[8] See above, Chapter VI.

9 See above, Chapter II.
10 e.g. by P. Huizing in *Le Lien Matrimonial*.
11 *Ibid.*, pp. 139-40, 141-2.
12 e.g. J. Dominian in *Christian Marriage*, p. 240, *Marital Break-down*, and *Marriage, Divorce and the Church*, Appendix 6. J. Bernhard in 'A propos de l'indissolubilité du mariage chrétien' in *Mémorial du Cinquantenaire 1919–1969* (Strasbourg).
(I am indebted to Professor Dunstan for drawing my attention both to this article and to the collection *Le Lien Matrimonial*.)
13 e.g. by J. Dominian.
14 In *Mémorial du Cinquantenaire 1919–1969*.
15 Cf. G. R. Dunstan, 'The Marriage Covenant', published in *Theology*, May 1975.
16 See above, pp. 57-8.
17 See above, Chapter VI, especially pp. 62ff.
18 Paragraphs 129-132.
19 Appendix 3, p. 122.
20 *Ibid.*, pp. 122-3.
21 John Lucas, 'Frustration and Forgiveness', *Theology*, May 1971, p. 200.
22 See *Marriage, Divorce and the Church*, Appendix 5, p. 131. J. L. Austin, 'Performative utterances' printed in *Philosophical Papers*, ed. J. D. Urmson and G. J. Warnock, and *How to do things with Words*.
23 Cf. *Marriage, Divorce and the Church*, Appendix 5, p. 138.
24 Cf. David Millar's appraisal of *Marriage, Divorce and the Church*, printed in *Crucible*, November–December 1972.
25 See above, p. 58.
26 Appendix 5, p. 136.
27 *Marriage, Divorce and the Church*, Appendix 3, p. 122.
28 *Ibid.* Appendix 5, p. 136.
29 May 1971.
30 p. 194.
31 *Ibid.*
32 p. 198.
33 p. 194.
34 *Marriage, Divorce and the Church*, Appendix 1, by Hugh Monte-fiore, Bishop of Kingston.
35 See above, p. 73.
36 *Marriage, Divorce and the Church*, Introduction, p. xii.
37 John Lucas, *Theology*, May 1971, p. 196.
38 See above, pp. 62-3.
39 *Theology*, May 1971, p. 200.
40 *Ibid.*, p. 199.
41 p. 197.
42 *Ibid.*
43 *Ibid.*, p. 199.

IX. DANGERS AND HOPES

1 November 1974.
2 November 24th, 1974.
3 'Bishop Leonard complained that it [*Marriage, Divorce and the Church*] was not a balanced summary of the matter and of views deeply and conscientiously held . . . but a brief pleading of a particular view of scripture and of the nature of marriage designed to obtain particular answers'—from the *Church Times* account (November 15th, 1974) of the debate in the General Synod, which was fuller than the Synod Report (Vol. 4.3).
4 *Marriage, Divorce and the Church*, p. xii.
5 *New Dimensions*, Appendix C, paragraph 17 (and the body of the report, paragraph 301).
6 *New Dimensions*, paragraph 283.
7 *Ibid.*, paragraph 333.
8 *Ibid.*, Appendix C, paragraph 3.
9 *Ibid.*, Appendix C, paragraph 4.
10 *The Sermon on the Mount*, p. 29.
11 *Ibid.*
12 *A Celebration of Faith*, p. 136.
13 *The Sermon on the Mount*, p. 29.
14 I have enlarged on this theme in an article called 'Head and Members' printed in *The Sacred Ministry*, ed. G. R. Dunstan.
15 See above, p. 95. Cf. *Putting Asunder*, paragraph 103.
16 Cf. *Marriage, Divorce and the Church*, Appendix 5, p. 136.
17 Cf. St. Augustine, *Confessions*, x 29.
18 *New Dimensions*, Appendix C, paragraph 15.

INDEX

109

110